My

Goodness!

REASONABLE HOLINESS

ISBN-13: **979-8499166444**
ISBN-10: **8499166444**

Scripture Quotations

Scripture quotations used in this book are from the following versions:

GNB – Good News Bible. Copyright © by The British & Foreign Bible Society, used by permission.

KJV – King James Version

MSG – The Message (Eugene H Peterson) Copyright © 1993, 1994, 1995, 1996, 2000, 2001, 2002. Used by permission of NavPress Publishing Group

NIV – New International Version. Copyright © by International Bible Society, used by permission of Hodder & Stoughton Ltd, a member of the Hodder Headline Group.

NLT – New Living Translation. Copyright © by Tyndale House Publishers Inc., used by permission.

i

CONTENTS

God's aim isn't to crush us with guilt – ignore Satan's false accusations – memory isn't reliable – the unforgivable sin – ups and downs – Grace isn't rationed and doesn't run out. – don't let guilty feelings continue unchecked.

1. Reasonable Holiness

Holiness is relevant to the Church's mission – it's meant to be the normal state of God's people – the meaning of holiness – Holiness makes sense – it isn't about forbidding activities – it's a relevant, reasonable, and worthwhile goal.

Holiness has become a rarely used word, even in Christian circles. It's gone out of fashion. Does that matter? Is holiness reasonable and relevant for today? Do we want it? Is it achievable?

Although we may be shy of talking about holiness, every so often we recognise and admire individuals who seem to have that special something. They may not be in influential positions, but they seem somehow to change the world around them. The Church doesn't necessarily warm to such people until after they die, as if sainthood shouldn't be permitted for the living. However, when the New Testament apostles addressed their letters, they freely applied the word 'saint' to ordinary members of local churches. The Greek word they used was 'hagios', which means 'holy', so holiness was a noted feature of those early churches. Why not now?

The Church in the western world has had an easy ride for several centuries, but there's no guarantee that it will stay like that. When the early Church faced persecution, their goodness was respected by ordinary people[1], if not by rulers, and that gave believers some protection. Under present day regimes that persecute Christians, believers are usually forbidden from talking about their faith, nevertheless their holy lives wordlessly

1

proclaim the Gospel. Do we need persecution to drive us to holiness?

Many Christians long for revival (and I pray for it myself) but what are we really hoping for? Do we suppose that revival will turn the tide in our favour, preventing future persecution? That may be a false hope because revival often comes amidst trials. Are we hoping for political power? full churches? rousing songs? happy, smiling faces? Or are we looking at it from God's viewpoint? Revival is firstly about purifying the Church, which means you and me – so why not begin the purification ahead of time? Do you want revival? Then be revived! Holiness is meant to be the normal state of God's people.

John Calvin said:

> 'God, after freely bestowing his grace on us, forthwith demands of us a reciprocal acknowledgement. When he said to Abraham, "I am thy God", it was an offer of his free goodness; but he adds at the same time what he required of him; "Walk before me, and be thou perfect,"

So how does our goodness measure up to that?

That Greek word, 'hagios' translates into Latin as 'sanctus' from which we get our words 'saint' and 'sanctification' (the process of becoming holy). People may be shy about the word 'holiness', but sanctification is accepted doctrine. The usual teaching is that conversion is an *event*, but sanctification is a *process* that develops over years. Does that mean that the only route to holiness is to grow old? Maybe your youthful years are already in the past, and you wonder whether this train has already left the station. Perhaps your past contains missed opportunities, broken promises, sad regrets and even some disillusionment. But there's no need to sit in a back pew nursing your disappointment. If you're still alive there is hope.

There may be times when an accusing voice suggests that your faith is weak, or that it's a sham (you speak the language of Christianity, and attend the meetings, but what about that past sin? What about those feelings of boredom or reluctance?). When that happens, it's time to reason with yourself.

> *"Come now, and let us reason together, saith the LORD: though your sins be as scarlet, they shall be as white as snow; though they be red like crimson, they shall be as wool."* [2]

Use a bit of memory and simple common sense. You remember how you became a Christian. You know the kind of life you have lived since then. You also know what you really want, deep in your heart. Satan (the name means *Accuser*) may use truths to create self-doubt, so you can use truths to reassure yourself and keep moving on with God. Would you really like to be holy? That is a reasonable aim.

> *"I beseech you therefore, brethren, by the mercies of God, that ye present your bodies a living sacrifice, holy, acceptable unto God, which is your **reasonable** service."* [3]

I choose that word *"Reasonable"* to title this chapter and to subtitle the whole book. I chose it because of the Bible verse you just read – *"your **reasonable** service"* – and its context of giving our bodies (i.e., our whole self, because everything we are is contained within our body). However, the word *reasonable* is sometimes taken to imply other meanings. Some may think of it as *moderation*, but there's nothing moderate about holiness. *Reasonable* sometimes seems to imply safety, but holiness is risky; search the Bible for references to holy places, things, or beings and it often comes with fear and danger. When a holy angel appears in the story, almost the first thing the angel says is *"don't be afraid"* – because the people *are* frightened. Holiness is a characteristic mark of the *Holy* Spirit, which identifies us to the enemy as prime targets for attack. No! Holiness is not safe, weak, boring, or moderate. So, let me make my point simply. By using the word *reasonable*, I mean:

HOLINESS
MAKES
SENSE

Stay with me on this, because it can change your life, your church, and the world around you.

Having read this far, you may be worrying that this book is advocating a return to medieval-style penances, or puritan-style restrictions (forbid dancing, ban Christmas, restrict fashion choices, keep a tight check on laughter and fun). These kinds of distortion bring holiness into disrepute. This is not an 'ought to' book, telling you what you should or shouldn't be doing. You know right from wrong, and the fact that you even opened the book suggests that your desire is to be the best for God. This book is about hope, aspiration, adventure, victory, enjoyment, and some down-to-earth ideas for continuing the journey along the narrow (but scenic) pathway of faith. Holiness is a desirable objective, a practical aim and (I hope to persuade you) it is a relevant, reasonable, and worthwhile goal. Only at the end will you know how close or how often you reached that goal, but the journey is a not-to-be-missed adventure.

"... I always try to maintain a clear conscience before God and all people." [4]

---

[1] *Acts 2:47*
[2] *Isaiah 1:18 (KJV)*
[3] *Romans 12:1 (KJV)*
[4] Acts 24:16 (NLT)

2. Faith or Works?

Jesus advocated righteous living – so did St. Paul – keeping these doctrines in balance – Holiness is powered by Divine Grace but requires human commitment.

Jesus gave the wrong answer. The rich young man asked a sincere question and expected a helpful response. He was impressed with the Galilean's preaching and wanted to do what's right. The question was, "*What must I do to inherit eternal life?* " [1], and the orthodox answer should have been something like, "*Follow me*", or "*Believe in me*". But Jesus said, "*You know the commandments...?*" and told the young man to abandon his wealth and give to the poor. What kind of evangelism was that? You would expect Jesus to know the Gospel!

Jesus often gave wrong answers. Where orthodox teaching talks doctrine, he continually talked about righteousness. Jesus said,

> "*...just as you can identify a tree by its fruit, so you can identify people by their actions. 'Not everyone who calls out to me, 'Lord! Lord!' will enter the Kingdom of Heaven. Only those who actually do the will of my Father in heaven will enter.*" [2]

And the apostles continued his teaching – including Paul, whose letters provide the best-known proof texts for the doctrine of 'justification by faith'. Yet even Paul constantly reminds his readers of the need to live righteously.

What's does this mean? Do Christians really need a reminder to do good? Evidently Paul thought so. He travelled widely through the Roman empire and knew very well the moral level of the societies they were living in. There were temptations all around them – including practises that were so entrenched in the communities that it could be dangerous *not* to engage in them. Idolatry was pervasive, and to stand aside from its ceremonies could result in losing your job or being otherwise punished. Even today in the West it may sometimes be costly to take a moral stand. But to compromise is to spoil our testimony. The gospel message is preached more effectively by actions than by words. Paul said, *"Therefore, since we have these promises, dear friends, let us purify ourselves from everything that contaminates body and spirit, perfecting holiness out of reverence for God."* [3] That quotation is typical of many in Paul's letters. So, how can we reconcile these contrasting elements of the apostle's teaching?

A stumbling block to talking about holiness is the apparent conflict between teachings about faith and good works. The Gospel message is emphatic that we are saved by Grace through faith. But we also understand that Christians are expected to live righteously. However, we may hesitate to say too much about good works in case we might be accused of casting doubt on the doctrine of salvation *"by faith alone"* [4], but Grace changes the story. By faith we receive free salvation, but Grace does more than grant forgiveness – it produces good works:

> *"For we are God's handiwork, created in Christ Jesus to do good works, which God prepared in advance for us to do."* [5]

Like a butterfly emerging from a chrysalis, those who have been saved by Grace have entered a new world. No longer earthbound, we have the freedom to fly. No longer confined, like caterpillars, to gorging on bitter leaves, we have acquired a taste for sweet nectar. Everything has changed. We are a new creation[6]. So, now we must learn to inhabit this new world.

It's not easy to fly when you're weighed down by preconceptions. Martin Luther was uncomfortable with the biblical letter of James because it seemed to contradict the doctrine of justification by faith. Luther was wrong, but understandably so. He had seen the results of false doctrines that told people they could earn salvation by good deeds or, more perniciously, by buying documents called 'indulgences' (a lucrative money-making scheme promoted by corrupt church officials). But James wasn't denying that Grace is free. Nor did Jesus get it wrong in the story that started this chapter. Jesus saw through the rich young man's enthusiasm and knew that it wouldn't last. Enthusiasm is not faith. In the parable of the sower, some seed fell among thorns, representing those people who heard his message and seemed to believe, but not with the kind of faith that would change their lives. Real faith is not just words. It produces changed lives – lives that continue changing – and, if the changes are real, they will be evident – as James said in his letter:

> *"How can you show me your faith if you don't have good deeds? I will show you my faith by my good deeds."* [7]

We don't gain anything by replaying the arguments of the Reformation. We know that justification is by Grace through faith. But the New Covenant was always intended to produce a fundamental life change:

> *"This is the covenant I will make with the people of Israel after that time,' declares the Lord. 'I will put my law in their minds and write it on their hearts. I will be their God, and they will be my people."* [8]

We should expect changed lives following conversion, and we should expect further changes as time goes by. Forgiveness is instant, but sanctification is a progressive process. Laws and commandments are signposts to righteousness, but *"no one will ever be made right with God by obeying the law"* [9]. Holiness is powered by divine Grace, but it requires human commitment. For instance, God will speak to us as we read the Bible, but we have to turn the pages for ourselves! The Holy Spirit will inspire us to do things, go places, communicate with people, but we have to put on our own shoes, drive our own cars, and generally make our own efforts to do his bidding. Faith is expressed in action.

These arguments matter because there have been people, sects, and leaders who brought the faith into disrepute, either by laxity leading to immorality or, on the other hand, by legalism leading to oppression. Faith and good works are aspects of the same great Truth, that must be kept in balance. We cannot do anything to earn our salvation or our ongoing forgiveness, but we are responsible to *work out* our salvation *"with fear and trembling"* [10]

By writing this book, am I implying that I have reached the goal of holiness? Certainly not! I write as one who is on the way, looking towards the goal, and praying for strength to continue to the end. As Paul said:

> *"I'm not saying that I have this all together, that I have it made. But I am well on my way, reaching out for Christ, who has so wondrously reached out for me. Friends, don't get me wrong: By no means do I count myself an expert in all of this, but I've got my eye on the goal, where God is beckoning*

us onward – to Jesus. I'm off and running, and I'm not turning back." [11]

I have done, thought, read, watched, heard, said, and shouted things for which I afterwards became ashamed. I repented of those things and received God's forgiveness. But each time, when God's Grace brought me back, it also impressed on me what I really want. Little by little, those experiences taught me that Grace offers more than forgiveness. In a sense, I was ashamed of needing forgiveness. I knew that if I sinned again, He would forgive me again, but deeper desires were urging me in a better direction. I wanted more and more to live out God's will. Sanctification – the process of becoming holy – is God's will for us, and Grace is the power that drives it.

---

[1] *Mark 10:17*

[2] *Matthew 7:20-21 (NLT)*

[3] *2 Corinthians 7:1 (NIV)*

[4] *N.B. the word "alone" does not appear in the Greek text of Romans 3:28. Martin Luther who interpolated that word into his German translation of the New Testament. To justify the insertion he asserted that it made the meaning clearer.*

[5] *Ephesians 2:10 (NIV)*

[6] *See 2 Corinthians 5:17*

[7] *James 2:18 (NLT)*

[8] *Jeremiah 31:33 (NIV)*

[9] *Galatians 2:16 (NIV)*

[10] *Philippians 2:12*

[11] *Philippians 3:12-14 (MSG)*

3. Defining holiness

To be holy is to be special — the word may attract negative connotations, but it is practical — wholeness — Christ's sacrifice was once for all — we are called to be citizens of the Kingdom of God

'Holy', and its associated word, 'holiness', are among the more frequently used words in the Bible. Both the Old Testament Hebrew word (*quodosh*) and its equivalent in New Testament Greek *(hagios)* carry the sense of something set apart. To be holy is to be special, like the best room in the house that's kept clean and tidy for visitors. Those who are holy are set apart for the Kingdom of God, which runs by different rules and standards than the nations of this world. When James and John, backed by their mother, asked Jesus to grant them a special place in his future kingdom[1], they were thinking in earthly terms. Their ambitions were not holy, but the fact that they got it wrong on that occasion didn't stop them from later committing themselves to be set apart to serve in the true Kingdom of God.

What words come to your mind when holiness is mentioned? For many people, the word conjures up such negative associations as:

- Pride
- Arrogance
- Rigidity
- Haughtiness
- Judgemental
- Self-satisfied
- Hypocritical

13

there are sound reasons for making those connections. We have probably all met religious people whose behaviour brought those images to mind. Such people demonstrate a false 'holiness', which is defined by things we are not allowed to do, rather than genuine, life-affirming goodness. Their version of holiness involves rising above the everyday world and keeping their distance from reality.

You might suppose that the word 'holy' would appear in the earliest pages of the Bible, but its first mention in Scripture doesn't come until Exodus – the second book. The word appears in the story of Moses and the burning bush. Moses probably saw many burning bushes as he led his flocks through the scorching desert. Under the burning desert sun it doesn't take much to set a dry thorn bush on fire. But this bush didn't shrivel to ashes as Moses expected – it kept burning. That's what made him turn aside to gaze in wonder. Then, as he approached the phenomenon, he heard a Voice coning from the fire, saying, *"...Take off your sandals, for the place where you are standing is holy ground."* [2]. By telling him to take his shoes off, the Voice was calling Moses to get *closer* to the earth (meaning *closer* to the needs of the people) – and then God sent him to rescue the Israelites from slavery. Holiness implies separation from evil deeds and selfish ambitions – but not from ordinary people, and not from practical service.

Moses' call to holiness was a call to get involved with human needs. Equally today, holiness doesn't mean that we should shut ourselves off from the world. If we were to separate ourselves from the ordinary people of

this world, we wouldn't be able to fulfil the Gre..
Commission[3]. We belong in the communities of the
world, but we shouldn't conform to their moral
standards.

> *"And be not conformed to this world: but be ye transformed
> by the renewing of your mind, that ye may prove what is that
> good, and acceptable, and perfect, will of God."* [4]

> *Being "not conformed" doesn't mean the no drinking, no
> dancing, no movies kind of nonconformity. No! That the
> kind of blanket moral hypocrisy has brought holiness a bad
> name. We each belong to different communities. In fact,
> many of us spend our lives in several different communities –
> our workplace, our neighbourhood, our care home, our
> school, our church, our sports club – and we need to make
> individual decisions about what we will accept and when we
> will hold back. Those decisions must be made in the light of
> our citizenship in the Kingdom of God.*

Many people think that holiness means living without
sin. That's too extreme an interpretation in one sense
and too narrow in another sense. There's another word
– wholeness – that better expresses the breadth of
meaning that we need. The Weald and Downland
Living Museum, in southern England, aims to rescue
and conserve historic buildings and to teach traditional
trades and crafts. Part of its work has been featured in
a BBC television programme called "The Repair Shop",
which shows skilled artisans fixing broken and worn-
out, but valued and memorable items brought in by
members of the public. It's a treat to see the skill of the
experts and the amazing transformations they achieve –
a leather satchel handmade in a First World War trench
but now looking dry and shrivelled – a porcelain vase,
formerly treasured by a long dead mother but shattered
in an accident – a grandfather clock, which was a valued

stopped working a generation ago – these
arently hopelessly damaged treasures were
or restoration. In each case, the artisans
saw the sorry condition of the goods and
believed in their potential. Then, they lovingly restored
them to beauty and usefulness. That's how Jesus deals
with us. Damaged and worn though we may be, he
believes in us, and commits to healing our brokenness
and giving us abundant life – wholeness.

True holiness is relevant to everyday life. It's earthy.
It's positive. It makes the world a better place. The
holiness that we seek is not that of a lonely retreat into
privacy and seclusion, though prayer can be as much a
way of involving ourselves with human needs as more
obvious practical acts. To pray effectively for a
community, we need to learn about it. Holiness gives.
In short, holiness is *practical* and *useful*. Yes, it does
include prayer in privacy and seclusion, but always with
a consciousness of a world to be saved. Holiness is
doing God's will and submitting our will to his. It is a
product of the life that grows in us, which Paul
described as the *'fruit of the spirit'* – but we'll return to
that subject in a later chapter.

The Gospel is good news for all people. It makes a
difference to those who have received forgiveness and
salvation. It makes a difference to those who benefit
from the renewed lives of those who Christ has
redeemed. In the words of the old hymn, "*He died that
we might be forgiven. He died to make us good*" [5]. The
theology of that hymn may be simplistic, but it carries
an important principle. Justification brings immediate
assurance of forgiveness as we repent. Sanctification is

the ongoing objective of justification. Let's be clear about this. Forgiveness doesn't have to be paid for again. Jesus paid the price in full. The very first sin you ever committed was in the distant future when Jesus went to the Cross. His sacrifice was once and for all – and for all time.

> *"As a priest, Christ made a single sacrifice for sins, and that was it!"* [6]

This is a great and wonderful mystery, and a cause for our everlasting gratitude – gratitude that continually drives our response. Our confessions don't alter God's attitude to us, but ours to him. He doesn't change, but we do.

Now there's room for confusion in this. If we separate the command to *'purify ourselves'* from the promise of fruitfulness, we place ourselves in a negative position. We will be trying to empty ourselves of bad things, rather than allowing the Holy Spirit to fill us with good things. Emptiness creates a vacuum, which will try to fill itself – but not necessarily with the good that we hope for. Wholeness, completeness, or fullness is what we seek. When the vessel is full, nothing else can get in. By the Grace and power of the Holy Spirit, the Lord offers us a positive kind of righteousness – the fruit that the Spirit nurtures in us as we look after the soil of our life and protect the faith that God has planted in us. Our calling is to be citizens of the Kingdom of God, living in obedience, sustained by his power – and that's the point of this book.

> *"Because we have these promises, dear friends, let us cleanse ourselves from everything that can defile our body or spirit. And let us work toward complete holiness because we fear God."* [7]

[1] Matthew 20:20-23
[2] Exodus 3:5 (NIV)
[3] Matthew 28:19,20
[4] Romans 12:2 (KGV)
[5] From the hymn, "There is a green hill far away"
[6] Hebrews 10:12 (MSG)
[7] 2 Corinthians 7:1 (NLT)

4. MY goodness!

The temptation to compare ourselves with others – the mote and the beam – know yourself – "us" and "them" – don't slavishly follow leaders down the wrong path – righteous living is part of evangelism.

> Peter turned round and saw behind him that other disciple, whom Jesus loved — the one who had leaned close to Jesus at the meal and had asked, "Lord, who is going to betray you?" When Peter saw him, he asked Jesus, "Lord, what about this man?" [1]

Peter did it. Many people have done it. Maybe you have done it too. When the spotlight shines on your life and behaviour, do you feel the urge to deflect it away by pointing to someone else? *"I may have been driving a bit over the limit but look how many cars passed me!"*

Holiness matters for everyone, but we are ultimately responsible only for our own lives. I called this book "*My Goodness!*" because that's the limit of its objective – me, the writer, and you, the reader. You and I are engaged in a private conversation. It concerns nobody but us. You are allowed to criticise me because I've had the audacity to raise the subject. But don't stand in judgement on anybody else. If you've been a Christian for long, and especially if you started hearing gospel stories as a child, you will surely recall what Jesus said about the man with a speck of dust in his eye, and the other man with a big plank sticking out from his face (traditionally, "the mote and the beam"). Don't even think about judging someone else unless you have dealt with your own issues.

On one occasion, some religious leaders thought they really had Jesus cornered. They brought him a woman who, so they said, had been caught in bed with a man who wasn't her husband. They were on firm legal ground. The Jewish Law made it clear that a woman caught in that situation should be executed by stoning (a horrible way to die). But they wanted to show that Jesus was soft on law breakers. If he failed to condemn the woman, they may be able to bring a charge against him, or at least they would blacken his name. If he condemned her, he might lose credibility with his followers. Jesus caught them off guard by saying, *"Whoever hasn't ever done anything wrong should throw the first stone."* [2] It was an effective foil to their cunning, and a lesson for us to take to heart. The hypocrisy of the people who brought this poor woman to Jesus leaps out of the story. If, as they alleged, she was caught *'in the very act'* of adultery, then they must also have seen the man who was with her. But they didn't bring him for judgement. Was the accusation true? Was it even nearly true? And if it were, how could the accusers expect to get away with double standards – one rule for the woman and a different one for the man? Jesus saw through their deceit and their hard-heartednes and settled the matter by shaming them.

We do well to know ourselves, which is surprisingly hard to do. I think that it's easier to know God than to know our own heart, because most of us learn early in life to hide our true selves from others – and we get so good it that we even hide from ourselves. We can each benefit by unearthing the things we have hidden, so that God can heal our deepest wounds. However, my weaknesses and vulnerabilities arise from my own background, genetic inheritance, upbringing, or life experiences – and I have no right to judge others who may be free to act differently from me – and to set different boundaries than I do. Ultimately, the life I must give account for is my own.

What responsibility do we have for the morals of the society we live in? For the first 300 years of the Christian Church, this question could only be answered in the secret place of prayer. Christians had no political power. They were despised, oppressed, and often persecuted. Roman society was pagan. It valued bravery above what we would consider as morality. It allowed parents to kill female children at birth, legalised the oppression and killing of slaves, subjugated women, and tolerated sexual exploitation. Christians didn't like these things, but they had no power to change the laws, or even to campaign against these evils. What they could do, was to live righteously – and that made them surprisingly influential. From the time of Constantine and onwards, the Church began to acquire power – and it didn't always use it well. Power compromised the Church and made it more difficult to discern between true disciples and nominal Christians. Laws began to reflect 'Christian morality' but were sometimes applied in oppressive ways that bore none of the marks of Christian love or mercy. That's how matters continued through many centuries in Europe (and in European colonies) producing witch-finders and heresy-hunters, inquisitions and pogroms. These behaviours have nothing to do with holiness.

We all know what a bird looks like. Whatever your artistic skills, if you pick up a pencil and sketch one from memory, the chances are that it will resemble the above picture, capturing the classic image that we associate with the word 'bird'. But we know many examples of the 'bird' category that don't fit the classic image. Think of penguins, kiwis, and ostriches. Humans often think in categories, which is why we find it so easy to *pre-judge* matters – we have *prejudices*. Holiness is not about conforming to an artificial standard of normality. Christian morality doesn't equate with mainstream, middle-class, averagely acceptable values. In pre-modern, village-based society it was easy to exclude people who didn't fit the acceptable norm. People could be banished from the community, isolated on the fringes or, in the worst cases, persecuted or killed. We like to think that our society has advanced since those times but, when cultures clash, prejudices come to the surface – and there's nothing holy about prejudice.

Just an aside for your comfort – flashes of prejudice are normal. They become unhealthy when we let them dictate our behaviour. I can recall occasions when, on first meeting a person, I felt negative responses rising up in me. I hadn't met these people before but was already making judgements about them. Why? My brain was checking them against a 'template' formed by past experiences of people I had known (possibly even childhood experiences). Something about their physical appearance, their way of moving, or their manner of speech, seemed to match the template and raised a 'be careful' alarm – but I learnt to reserve my judgement, and those people became good friends. Our animal responses to new situations are there for our protection, and there's no shame in that. We just need to reason with ourselves and watch for other signs. Classifying people on the basis of their surface characteristics is dangerous. Make righteous judgements.

The classic 'pharisaic' attitude to holiness is to condemn 'them' and take pride in being 'one of us'. By that means, those who view themselves as 'holier than thou' can boost their self-assurance by looking for things to condemn. In its extremes, this attitude can become hateful, and even violent, because the most hated objects become victims of persecution. In my lifetime, society has persecuted unmarried mothers (but not fathers), people with mental illness, divorced women (but usually not divorced men) and people of different race or colour. In earlier ages, to be an old woman living alone was to risk persecution as an alleged witch. We may feel uncomfortable about the morality of some people's lifestyle, but judgement is God's prerogative. We don't become holier by condemning other people.

We don't become holier by mindlessly obeying other people either, so beware of following bad or unwise leaders, whether in secular or church society. When you stand at the judgement seat of Christ[3] how will you respond to questions like:

- Why did you do that?
- Why did you say that?

- Why did you go along with the crowd when they did that?

Will it be acceptable to say, "*They* told me to do that/say that/go along with that"? We can't blame our choices on other people, however senior, powerful, or respected they may be. We are individually responsible for what we do. Be warned. There are cults and individuals who try to pressurise their followers to accept rules that go against individual conscience. The errors of some of these cults are obvious to everyone except the most thoroughly brain-washed devotees, but every cult starts by being plausible. And good people can also make mistakes. On one occasion, the apostle Paul, had to rebuke even the most senior of his fellow apostles – Peter – for changing his behaviour to appease some false teachers who had come from Jerusalem[4].

My wife and I were on our way to bed when the doorbell rang. Cautiously, we went to the front door, then opened it to our friends, Pete and Janet[5]. They and we were members of a 1970s 'House Church'. Janet, a Primary School Teacher and Pete, Company Secretary for a prominent local business, were devoted to God and to each other – but they weren't yet married. After an evening out, Pete took Janet back to her apartment and found it locked and bolted (Janet's flatmate must have thought that she was already home and in bed). Could we put Janet up for the night? Yes, of course we could. As Pete drove away Janet burst into tears and told us the whole story. Pete lived in an apartment above the company offices, but it wouldn't seem right for Janet to sleep there. He also had access to an adjoining, unoccupied flat that she could have

used – but they wanted to *abstain from all appearance of evil*
[6]. However, the reason for Janet's distress was that the
fellowship elders were trying to stop them from
marrying. Pete asked them if it was because he'd been
married before (years earlier, his wife had been
unfaithful, deserted him, and persuaded him to
divorce). No, the elders said, it wasn't the divorce.
Was it because of the age difference? The elders said
no. Then why? They simply asserted that they didn't
believe that marriage was right for that couple.

Think about this proposition. There was no
implication of immorality (the couple's behaviour that
night was a demonstration of their moral stand). If the
marriage went wrong, who would pay the price?
Certainly not the elders! They were *forbidding to marry*[7]
without giving a reason, and they had ordered the
couple to stop seeing one another or to leave the
church.

The couple were noticeably absent from the next
fellowship meeting, so I spoke up.

"Where are Pete and Janet?"

"We'd rather you didn't ask!"

"Why have they been banned from coming?"

"Please, just leave it there!"

So, I opened my Bible at Matthew's Gospel and read
the instructions Jesus gave for dealing with conflict in
the church:

> *"If your brother or sister sins, go and point out their fault,*
> *just between the two of you. If they listen to you, you have*
> *won them over.*
>
> *But if they will not listen, take one or two others along, so*
> *that 'every matter may be established by the testimony of two*
> *or three witnesses.'*

25

If they still refuse to listen, tell it to the church; and if they refuse to listen even to the church, treat them as you would a pagan or a tax collector." [8]

It is right under some circumstances for people to be put out of the church, but not without proper examination, and not in secret. My intervention was not well received, and it wasn't long before my wife and I were also put out of the church.

That outcome wasn't surprising, but they went further. They told other members not to speak to us, but to cut off all contact. We noticed some of them crossing the street to avoid us. But we trusted the Lord to resolve these matters, knowing that we had not compromised our faith or our commitment to love. In that confidence we were able to forgive those who had harmed us, and to take every opportunity to show kindness to them. That local church group was part of a much larger movement that temporarily went off the rails, prompting exaggerated teachings about discipleship. Key leaders in that movement later recognised their error and abandoned heavy-handed leadership. The local fellowship also relented – and some of them are now among our close friends, although we now happen to live a long distance apart. They also renewed their friendship with Pete and Janet (who were happily married for over 30 years).

Give due honour to leaders and pay attention to what they say – but don't slavishly follow them down a wrong path. We are individually accountable for our own words and deeds.

I have faced many moral choices in churches, in business, in family life, and in personal relationships, and the deciding factor is always "how will I account to God for my decision?" Sometimes the answer has led me to take a stand that brought criticism or misunderstanding. But my holiness is my responsibility. Each of us stands on our own account. Some moral decisions we must make will be difficult, or even costly. The Bible gives guidance on many issues, but we often face issues of this modern age that have little obvious precedent in Scripture. We now recognise conditions such as Asperger's, autism, Tourette's syndrome, and dyspraxia that cause people to behave in ways we may not understand. We now know that 'male' and 'female' are not such clear-cut distinctions as we used to imagine. What does this have to do with holiness? It affects how we judge ourselves and other people.

This is a difficult area for us. Undoubtedly, Christian campaigners have produced wonderful changes that vastly improved our society. We proudly look back on the movements that outlawed slavery (though the nations that abolished slavery had previously been actively involved in it). We applaud the improvements to prisons, the banning of child labour, and the provision of education for all. Most of these, and many other advances in our society owe their origins to Christian campaigners. But, though their social actions were praiseworthy, each one of them was ultimately accountable to God for the goodness of their personal lives.

- Is your local cinema showing films that you consider immoral?
- Does your local newsagent have pornographic magazines on the shelf?

- Does your local school teach things that conflict with your morals?

Questions like these are relevant to your evangelism, the protection of your children, or your care for your neighbours – but they have no direct relevance to your personal holiness. You don't make yourself righteous by frowning on other people's behaviour. If you are moved to campaign or speak about these issues, firstly (and honestly) check your motives for doing it. Make sure that you do it with compassion rather than condemnation. Demonstrate righteousness in love and mercy. What attitude did Jesus take to local scandals?

"the Pharisees and the teachers of the law muttered, "This man welcomes sinners and eats with them." [9]

Jesus didn't follow the kind of righteousness that the religious leaders expected. He found value in people who the Pharisees despised. Jesus focused instead on sincerity, and the willingness to change. Check on the occasions when Jesus spoke harshly and you will see that his anger was directed at the pompous and self-righteous, the proud and arrogant, rather than the people they looked down on as outcasts.

However, inner goodness doesn't mean that our righteousness should be invisible.
Jesus said:

"let your light shine before others, that they may see your good deeds and glorify your Father in heaven." [10]

Our good deeds come from inside – they proceed from our good intentions. Genuine good deeds are not done *in order* to be seen, nor *for the purpose of* earning favours. They are the product of inner holiness. But they are often noticed, even when nobody comments. Their testimony preaches the Gospel louder than our words.

Righteous living is part of evangelism, not because we talk about the Gospel, but because we *live* it.

So, let me ask you: have you reached perfection? Do you have unresolved issues that worry or concern you? Are you free from all the hang-ups that may have arisen through your childhood? Do you have habits that you wish you could break? Are you enjoying wholeness and peace? Those are the kinds of questions we must face on our journey of sanctification.

> *"It is God's will that you should be sanctified: that you should avoid sexual immorality; that each of you should learn to control your own body in a way that is holy and honorable, not in passionate lust like the pagans, who do not know God;"* [11]

> *"For God did not call us to be impure, but to live a holy life."* [12]

> *"Therefore, since we are surrounded by such a great cloud of witnesses, let us throw off everything that hinders and the sin that so easily entangles. And let us run with perseverance the race marked out for us, fixing our eyes on Jesus, the pioneer and perfecter of faith. For the joy set before him he endured the cross, scorning its shame, and sat down at the right hand of the throne of God."* [13]

It is our own holiness we must account for. Comparing ourselves with anyone else is self-deception. Jesus told a story about a respected community leader who went into a church and thanked God that he was better than other people. In particular, he thought himself better than the man he noticed in the opposite pew – a man with a bad reputation. But thanking God for his supposed goodness was false humility. He was basing his self-estimate on comparison with another man. When we are comparing ourselves with other people, and when we look down on them, we reveal the true level of our righteousness – we are seeking a low standard of comparison to make ourselves feel better than we are. God's standard is *"Be holy, because I am holy"*.

> *"So don't make judgments about anyone ahead of time—before the Lord returns. For he will bring our darkest secrets to light and will reveal our private motives. Then God will give to each one whatever praise is due."* [14]

---

[1] *John 20:20-21 (GNB)*

[2] *See John 8:1-11. Some scholars question whether this story was originally part of John's gospel, or whether it was added later. I am not qualified to judge that issue, but I believe the story to be consistent with the character and behaviour of Jesus as elsewhere portrayed in the New Testament.*

[3] *2 Corinthians 5:10*

[4] *Galatians 2:11-16*

[5] *This is a true story, but the names have been changed for the sake of confidentiality.*

[6] *1 Thessalonians 5:22*

[7] *1 Timothy 4:3*

[8] *Matthew 15:15-17 (NIV)*

[9] *Luke 15:2 (NIV)*

[10] *Matthew 5:16 (NIV)*

[11] *1 Thessalonians 4:3-5 (NIV)*

[12] *1 Thessalonians 4:7 (NIV)*

[13] *Hebrews 12:1-2 (NIV)*

[14] *1 Corinthians 4:5 (NLT)*

5. Fallen!

*Failure, despair, and forgiveness – free will means loving submission,
rather than enslavement –repentance always brings forgiveness –
progress does not follow a continuous upward slope.*

The Bible is so serious about holiness that it mentions it over 1000 times, but it doesn't spare the blushes of its heroes. Moses was a murderer (or a freedom fighter - the difference is only political). David was an adulterer. Jonah ran away from God's calling. Gideon was an idolater. Also, in the New Testament, the weaknesses of Mark, Peter, Paul, John, and many other saints are faithfully recorded. With the sole exception of Jesus, everyone failed. What about us?

Geoff slumped down on the settee, shaking. He wanted to cry, but tears wouldn't come – couldn't come. Anger was his most accessible emotion, but it left him feeling helpless. Now that it had subsided, he simply felt ashamed. He had lost control and lashed out – again. He had fallen from his own high standards and struck the person he most cared for. He knew it was wrong but couldn't help himself. Would he be forgiven? How could he break this repeated pattern of behaviour?

Chrissy liked a glass of wine when she got home from shopping. That is, she used to enjoy it, until one glass was no longer enough. Eventually, no amount of alcohol could fully ease her anguish.

Gemma's dependency arose from a genuine need. After breaking her ankle, she developed a chronic pain condition and needed strong painkillers to suppress the agony. Eighteen months later, pain was no longer her biggest problem – it was her dependence on the analgesics and the deceits she used to obtain them.

David was addicted to online gambling. It had started tamely enough, but now it ruled his life and devoured his income. His wife hadn't left him – yet.

James got into the habit of watching pornographic films. It started almost by accident when he chanced upon a link but, when it happened again several times, he admitted to himself that it was no longer accidental. It was becoming a habit – and he really wanted to break it.

These people were being controlled by repeated behaviours, in some cases amounting to addiction. Being an exaggerated condition, addiction shows up what's behind most repetitive sins. They often arise from inherent weaknesses in the victim. People who are subject to outbursts of anger, alcoholics, and sex addicts are driven by forces they can't understand, let alone control. But anger isn't necessarily a sin. As for alcohol, many people drink, but only a few become alcoholics. Sexual acts become sinful only when they are used outside the context of a loving relationship.

The above examples are not real, at least, not quite. They are composites of different people but, for each of them, there was forgiveness, a way out, and some important lessons. If a particular sin is becoming a habit, there's one simple answer – don't do it! Does that sound heartlessly simplistic? A later chapter of this book will go into detail about how we can overcome temptation, but here are some brief hints. If we try to fight temptation directly with willpower, we are keeping our focus on the temptation. A better solution is to change the subject, think about something different, or do something else – replacing the negative "don't" with positive action. If, after trying all that, you feel that it's really too much for you, just throw yourself on God – "*I can't do it, Lord. Help me!*". That works. But you will do even better if you can discover the root of your weakness.

Repeated behaviours are often indicators of a deeper problem that may be rooted in earlier life events. In childhood, especially, we may have had experiences that we couldn't understand. There may have been physical or sexual abuse, tragedy, neglect – or maybe incidents that were innocent in themselves, but which our infant minds misunderstood and misinterpreted. Such things may leave wounds long after we forget the original issues (or hide them in our unconscious mind). Finding the root of our behaviour doesn't excuse it, but it helps us understand why we need to set our boundaries tighter than other people find necessary.

Many Christians worry about their repeated behaviours – their habitual sins. Why, after living in God's truth, do we fall so often? The New Covenant gives us power to live righteously, but Christians retain free will. We have a spiritual motivation urging us forward in the direction of goodness, but we can resist the Spirit – or we can be caught unawares and trip over unexpected temptation. God gave us free will because he wants our relationship with him to be one of loving submission, rather than enslavement. Tyranny is the Devil's way. God's way is love. "*Love God, and do as you like*" is a partly misquoted version of one of St. Augustine's sayings (I didn't make it up!) Jesus said more-or-less the same thing, but he put it the other way round: "*If you love me keep my commandments*". Faced with that thought, it's no wonder that we sometimes despair of ourselves when we fall.

Peter asked Jesus, "...*how many times must I forgive my brother who sins against me*? [1] and suggested that seven times would be generous. In reply, Jesus proposed seventy times seven times. He didn't mean literally "*forgive him 490 times then go for his throat!*". He meant unlimited forgiveness because that's the standard he uses. No matter how many times we do wrong, when we come to God in repentance, he forgives – again and again. That's his nature. That's what Jesus paid for on the Cross. We are continually being given a fresh start – a clean slate. But it hurts us to know that fact. It feels devastating when, as we set out to do some good work, or some spiritual act, life interrupts with an unexpected challenge that triggers our anger, or selfishness, or whatever inappropriate response comes to us habitually. We feel hopeless! We've done it again!

Several times already in this book I've stated that God's Grace gives us the power to resist temptation. So then, how is it that we, who have received forgiveness can still fall into temptation? Gravity is such a powerful force that it holds planets, stars, and even mighty galaxies together. The power of gravity reaches right across the universe – but we can resist it simply by picking up a stone or leaping into the air. Nevertheless, we learn from childhood that gravity should be respected, because, when we fall, we get hurt. God's power is universal, but he doesn't impose it on us by force. We can resist. But it's wiser to submit.

There's a counterpart to limitless forgiveness. It is frequent confession, and it's a long-established spiritual principle. Setting out the Old Testament rules for forgiveness of sins, the Law says repeatedly, "*admit your guilt*" [2] ("*confess your sin*"). The principle behind all the sacrificial rites of the Hebrew Law was forgiveness. That principle carries through into the New Testament. If, after previous falls, we've 'done it again' we need to confess it again. Holding back and wallowing in the shame gets us nowhere. There's no point wasting time punishing ourselves because we think we deserve it. Maybe we do deserve punishment under strict judicial Law, but we're not under Law – we're under Grace [3]. Grace goes on forgiving and thereby piling an embarrassing sense of obligation on our shoulders. The more God forgives us, the more we want to show him our gratitude. That, over time, spurs us on to seek holiness.

If you find yourself becoming trapped in *repetitive* bad habits, a more formal confession can be useful. Confession, that is, to a trusted human. Some Protestants may feel uncomfortable about this type of confession, but it is thoroughly biblical:

> "*Therefore confess your sins to each other and pray for each other so that you may be healed. The prayer of a righteous person is powerful and effective.*" [4]

Confessing to God is essential, and brings forgiveness, but when you confess to a friend you take an important risk. Now your friend *knows*. Now he or she may *ask you* about it. Now he or she will *pray* for you. Who should you confess to? A righteous person. A person who will respect your confidentiality. A person with maturity. A person who cares about you. I've been on both sides of this matter, seeking prayer for myself, and praying with and for other people – and it does help. If someone seeks your prayer support in this way, listen sympathetically. When someone chooses to turn from sin, they know all about condemnation. They don't need to be reminded of it because they're weighed down by it. What they need is compassion and healing.

If you become trapped in a repetitive habit you may not feel able to free yourself. You will never break free until you accept that you have a problem but, once you admit your weakness, you will probably still need help. In the case of addictions to physical substances you may require medical intervention. Be determined. Be honest with yourself and with the people whose help you need. Be honest with God. Take hold of his promise:

> *"No temptation has overtaken you except what is common to mankind. And God is faithful; he will not let you be tempted beyond what you can bear. But when you are tempted, he will also provide a way out so that you can endure it."* [5]

Look for that way out – and use it.

Our desire for holiness makes us conscious of sin. In our awareness of sin, we may have some issues that we've been struggling with for a long time. Our damaged lives may be affected by long-term problems that point back to events early in our childhood. As infants, we were unable to rationalise everything that happened to us, so we adopted strategies for coping with our fears – sometimes unhealthy strategies. Such long-term issues may come to the surface as habitual sins – behaviours that we repeat over and over again. When we see that kind of pattern occurring, it's time to ask "*Why?*". What is the source of weakness that drives us to trip over the same obstacle time after time? In later chapters we'll look closer at the nature of temptation and how to overcome it.

However, our frustration with ourselves isn't always caused by sin. We may feel out-of-sorts for no obvious reason and start blaming ourselves for being down in the dumps. Don't despair. Progress never follows a continuous upward slope. The tide comes up the beach wave after wave, but each wave retreats before the next one. We're human. We have moods. You may be disappointed with yourself, but never give up hope. When you feel down, look up.

Most of us have times when we feel defeated, disappointed, or unworthy. Life sometimes tests us and throws us to the ground. Losing our jobs, falling out with friends or relations, being cheated, or rejected, missing a promotion, falling on hard times, suffering illness, losing a loved one – all kinds of setbacks may come our way and drive us to despair. So, we tell ourselves, "*I'm a Christian. I ought not to be in despair/depressed/unhappy. I've done it again!*" Don't let it get you down. The setbacks you suffer are real, and the pain shouldn't be denied. But those setbacks are the pressures that can mould you into the best that you can be.

It's not that God sends trials. Setbacks are part of life's variability. But when trying experiences come our way, the Lord walks through them with us, sometimes a step ahead of us – leading the way through. Does God ever leave us to get along on our own? Yes, he sometimes stands back just as human parents stand back at key points in their children's lives, like taking their first steps, setting off on their first bike, or climbing over obstacles. We know that our children's development depends on taking risks and learning to manage. But, oh how quickly we gather them up into our arms when they crash or fall! You may already be familiar with the poem "footsteps in the sand" (or "footprints" in some versions). I won't repeat it here but suggest that you encourage yourself by searching for it on the Internet. Whether it's our own sin, or some external problem that has come upon us, we need not be crushed by it. He is with us to win.

You don't have to be a loser. If circumstances seem stacked against you, get angry! You can fight back. Imagine that you're being attacked in your own home by a burglar. Sense your indignation, your fury, and your determination to protect yourself and eject the intruder. Channel the same kind of anger into resisting the spiritual/mental assault and committing your energy into achieving the holiness you desire. That's the battle that Paul described in a complex passage that I paraphrase as follows:

"I decide to act one way, but then I do the opposite – even doing things I deplore. That's why we need the Law. But it doesn't really work! I know the Law, but I can't be relied on to keep it because sin is so powerful that it overcomes my will. As soon as I decide to do good, sin pulls the rug from under my feet. I truly value righteousness, but it's obvious that some parts of me don't have the same standards. I've tried every way to resolve the problem, but nothing works. Is there anything or anyone who can help? YES! Jesus can

fix it!' [6]

When we feel that we can't cope we need to recognise and admit that we can't cope! At that point we surrender to God and call on him to act in us. He fights alongside us if we let him, and he equips us for the battle. That brings us to the well-known passage about the Armour of God[7], which famously doesn't include any protection for the warrior's back. Running away is not an option. Maybe you have fallen. Maybe the intruder got in because you left a (metaphorical) window open. But this is no time for retreating in despair and self-hatred. It's the time to fight back, gain control, and resolve to lock up properly in future.

We are in a war, and people get hurt in wars. Victory doesn't come cheaply. We win some; we lose some. But the ultimate end for the Kingdom of God is assured victory – a victory in which you and I are involved. Many of the battles are fought in our minds and in our bodies. For that reason, we need to allow the Holy Spirit to work through our own sanctified spirit to win over our minds and bodies, that is, to bring them to holiness. Taking a cue from Paul again, we need to bring our bodies into subjection[8].

> *"Don't you realize that in a race everyone runs, but only one person gets the prize? So run to win! All athletes are disciplined in their training. They do it to win a prize that will fade away, but we do it for an eternal prize. So I run with purpose in every step. I am not just shadowboxing. I discipline my body like an athlete, training it to do what it should. Otherwise, I fear that after preaching to others I myself might be disqualified."* [9]

No athlete achieves record pace after just one training session. Progress is interrupted by failures, and sometimes by injuries. Winners are people who fail, pick themselves up, start again, fail again, and still keep aiming for the target. Don't be beaten by your past, take deliberate steps to change things. If you have failed, begin your recovery by repentance (the subject of our next chapter) then use the experience to move forward with perseverance. Above all, remember that the only reason you have any hope of making progress is the Grace of God – but that's limitless.

[1] *Matthew 18:21 (NET)*
[2] *Leviticus 5:1-4*
[3] *Romans 6:14*
[4] *James 5:16 (NIV)*
[5] *1 Corinthians 10:13 (NIV)*
[6] *Summary based on Romans 7:15-25.*
[7] *Ephesians 6:11-18*
[8] *1 Corinthians 9:27*
[9] *1 Corinthians 9:24-27 (NLT)*

6. Repentance

Two kings sinned; one was condemned but the other was forgiven –
Why? – an analysis of the prayer of confession.

Saul and David were Israel's first two kings[1], but they were completely different personalities. However, there was something other than kingship that they had in common – they both committed notable sins and were publicly censured for their wrongdoing.

Saul's sin was disobedience – twice. Firstly, he intruded on the priests' office by offering a ritual sacrifice in a way that only anointed priests were allowed to do[2]. Secondly, he disobeyed a specific command from God. The Prophet Samuel instructed him, in God's name, to attack and annihilate the Amalekite nation and to destroy all their possessions. The Amalekites had been a threat to Israel for several generations and the realistic options for Israel were to destroy them or be destroyed by them. But Saul didn't do as he was told. He spared some of the Amalekites and brought back their possessions as booty.

David's great sin was a combination of adultery and murder (by proxy). While his army and his chief officers were away fighting a war, he stayed at home, where he had time on his hands. While strolling on the roof of his palace one evening, he noticed a woman bathing in a nearby garden, and he lusted after her. He called her to the palace, where she spent the night with him. Then, when she announced that she was pregnant, David instructed his army commander to place her husband in the front line of battle so that he would be killed.

41

Saul's disobedience was challenged by the prophet Samuel, who announced that, because of his behaviour, Saul would lose the kingdom. By contrast David, who was confronted by the prophet Nathan, remained king to the end of his long life. These contrasting outcomes seem inconsistent and unjust. By today's moral standards, David's lapse seems worse than Saul's. Some might say that, by declining to go through with genocide, Saul was in the right. But David's adultery and abuse of power could cause a modern political leader to be hounded by the media until he resigned.

Both men were found out, and both men were confronted and called to account by prominent prophets of God. However, they responded to those challenges in quite different ways. Saul made excuses and tried to shift the blame:

"Yes, you told me to destroy the Amalekites, and I did! Well, most of them anyway!"

"OK, you told me not to take any booty from the battle, but the soldiers brought these cattle back, and they only did it to make a sacrifice to the LORD!"

David's response was dramatically different. He acknowledged his sin. He broke down in tears and repented – and the text of his penitential prayer is preserved as Psalm 51, which serves as a model for true repentance. Much of the psalm may be familiar because it's been incorporated into other prayers. So, I am quoting it verse-by-verse from the less familiar Good News Bible version[3]:

1.Be merciful to me, O God, because of your constant love. Because of your great mercy wipe away my sins!

2. Wash away all my evil and make me clean from my sin!

Repentance is possible because God is not a tyrant. People who live under tyranny, whether political or domestic, yearn to throw off restraint, but people who know they are loved remain loyal. God's love and mercy throw light on our sin and make it look as bad as it really is. When we remember how good he is, we can't hide how wrong we have been, and we long to get back into his favour. We long to be clean.

3. I recognize my faults; I am always conscious of my sins.

True repentance recognises the reality of the sin and makes no attempt to cover or excuse it. It makes no appeal to extenuating circumstances, and no attempt to lessen the guilt. Total forgiveness depends on full and frank confession, and a determination not to do it again.

4. I have sinned against you — only against you — and done what you consider evil. So you are right in judging me; you are justified in condemning me.

In repentance we affirm that God is just. We recognise his right to punish us. How much sweeter then is the relief that we experience when we receive his forgiveness.

5. I have been evil from the day I was born; from the time I was conceived, I have been sinful.

The sins we fall into are often rooted in our inherent weaknesses and individual dispositions. We may have become vulnerable because of attitudes we learnt from our parents, from poor upbringing, from deprivation, or from traumatic events we experienced in childhood – but that's no excuse. Whatever we may have suffered in childhood, we remain responsible for what we do as adults. We do well to identify and understand our weakness, but we are presently and personally accountable for our thoughts, words, and actions. Whatever our circumstances, we always have a choice to do right or wrong. True repentance accepts responsibility.

6. *Sincerity and truth are what you require; fill my mind with your wisdom.*

Sincerity and truth – we know what the words mean, but we also know that sincerity doesn't always deliver success. That's why the psalm harnesses it to the word "truth". When we sincerely mean to change, we need also to recognise that the sin was not an accident. Whatever tripped us up also revealed our weakness. Human beings stand upright, which gives us some advantages, but makes us vulnerable to falling over. We put four legs on our tables and chairs because they stand up better that way. I love to walk in the countryside, over fields, and up hills and mountains. It's beautiful, and it's healthy, but there's a risk of slipping or tripping. That's why the psalmist asks for wisdom. In our walk of faith, we need to watch where we tread, and take due care. We sincerely mean not to fall again, but wisdom teaches us to be on our guard and take appropriate care. When we know that we're vulnerable, we learn to rearrange our lives to avoid repeating the same mistakes. As the book of Hebrews advises, "*Make level paths for your feet*" [4] – why make things difficult for ourselves?

7. Remove my sin, and I will be clean; wash me, and I will be whiter than snow.
8. Let me hear the sounds of joy and gladness; and though you have crushed me and broken me, I will be happy once again.

Sin hurts. Sin corrupts. Sin brings sorrow. Repentance is our way back to comfort, health, cleanness, and joy. The desire for good things is what drives us to repent. We may have been deceived by temptations to try quick, cheap pleasures and false gratification, but they always disappoint. The pleasures of sin don't last. They lead to further temptations and deeper disappointments. "*Sounds of joy and gladness*" come from the knowledge that we are whole, and clean – and that our heart does not condemn us[5].

9. Close your eyes to my sins and wipe out all my evil.
10. Create a pure heart in me, O God, and put a new and loyal spirit in me.

The Lord is keen to put our sins out of sight. "*He has removed our sins as far from us as the east is from the west.*" [6] When we pray for cleansing, our request will always be granted. As for creating a pure heart, we need that more than anything else in our journey towards a life of holiness. That's what Grace provides.

11. Do not banish me from your presence; do not take your Holy Spirit away from me.
12. Give me again the joy that comes from your salvation, and make me willing to obey you.

One of the most painful things that we feel when we know we have sinned is the loss of our sense of God's presence. It is possible to grieve the Holy Spirit [7], so that we lose that comforting sense of his closeness. In our prayer of repentance, we need to ask God to fill us again with his Spirit, so that we return to the fullness of his joy. His presence is our birth right. Constantly ask for it.

13. Then I will teach sinners your commands, and they will turn back to you.
14. Spare my life, O God, and save me, and I will gladly proclaim your righteousness.
15. Help me to speak, Lord, and I will praise you.

Repentance is not simply good for us, the ones who have confessed. It benefits the people we are in contact with. The burden of unconfessed sin clouds our testimony. Embarrassed by our faults, we no longer feel able to speak freely about God. Once we obtain forgiveness, we have a renewed lightness of heart, which shines out for others to see.

16. You do not want sacrifices, or I would offer them; you are not pleased with burnt offerings.
17. My sacrifice is a humble spirit, O God; you will not reject a humble and repentant heart.

Much of the book of Exodus, most of Leviticus, and significant portions of Numbers and Deuteronomy, describe sacrifices and offerings to be made by the Israelite priests. There was an elaborate system for obtaining forgiveness under the Old Covenant – and it involved a great deal of blood. The system of sacrifices was complex and detailed but, for many people, it deteriorated into mere ritual. People, especially wealthy people, used it as a way of buying their way out of trouble without actually changing their behaviour. They reasoned that they could oppress the poor, cheat in business, break the law, then go through the rituals to remove their guilt! It cost them a few sheep or cattle, but they could shrug their shoulders and carry on as before. It was a sham!

David recognised that God demanded something different. He recognised that sacrifices were merely symbolic. What God wanted was genuine repentance, meaning a change of direction. It's also easy to perform empty rituals in the name of Christianity. The Anglican "General Confession", and similar prayers from Roman Catholic and nonconformist traditions are used in churches week by week, but not always effectively. Even the words of this psalm can be used in vain. What matters is not the words we speak, but the truth we mean. Confession must never be a hollow formality.

18. O God, be kind to Zion and help her; rebuild the walls of Jerusalem.
19. Then you will be pleased with proper sacrifices and with our burnt offerings; and bulls will be sacrificed on your altar.

David's submission fully explains why he "got away with" his great crimes. It wasn't fair. God's mercy is never fair, because none of us really deserves forgiveness. God's Grace allowed a sinless man, Jesus, to be punished so that sinful people could go free. Christ's ignominious death is a price that can never be repaid – but Grace offers free acceptance.

Holiness is achievable if sin is quickly and fully repented. With the Holy Spirit's power, we can resist sin, and we can live in victory. But, when we do fall, we must put it behind us quickly, honestly, and thoroughly. That's the kind of sacrifice that brings joy to God and peace to us.

---

[1] *Saul's son, Ish Bosheth, reigned for a short time over part of the country, but his reign was simultaneous with David's rule, and wasn't counted in the line of succession.*
[2] *1 Samuel 13:7-14*
[3] *Psalm 51:1-19 (GNB)*
[4] *Hebrews 12:13 (NIV)*
[5] *1 John 3:20*
[6] *Psalm 103:12 (NLT)*
[7] *Ephesians 4:30*

7. Perseverance

Sanctification is not an event, but a process – encouragements help – Jesus recognised his own needs and made a point of maintaining his strength – Perseverance is not avoiding life's problems, but working through them.

Sanctification is not an event, but a process. It depends on God, but it requires our commitment. The Holy Spirit works in us continually, but he doesn't *force* us to change – he invites us. On our part, the inner force that moves us to respond may well be shame. We sense our unworthiness – the fact that we don't deserve his generosity – and may even feel separated from God, just as Adam felt in the Garden of Eden story [1]. The desire to be close to God propels us forward to be the best that we can be. However, we're never alone in this battle, nor does the outcome depend on our own abilities. The Holy Spirit provides strength and encouragement. During a weekend prayer retreat, I walked through the grounds of the retreat centre and discovered a small Chapel, half-hidden among the trees behind the main building. I listened at the door to check if it was occupied, then quietly slipped inside. I had things on my mind, and this seemed a good time to step aside and pray about it. During that period of my life, I was recognising emotional scars that originated from earlier disasters, but which still weighed me down (though I was starting to find healing). I often receive inspiration from dreams, but I've rarely experienced waking spiritual visions – but I did then. A clear vision formed in my mind. I saw a stone, more-or-less rectangular, but rounded at the corners and smoothed across much of the surface – but not the whole surface.

Later in the day I discussed the vision with the retreat leader.

"Where was Jesus in this vision? She asked.

The question surprised me, so I thought for a moment, then replied, *"He was watching"*

"And where were you?" was her next question.

*"I **was** the stone"*

"So what was Jesus doing?"

"He was smiling,"

Her gentle questioning helped me understand that God had given me the vision to encourage me. Years of battling with problems rooted in my childhood had already made a lot of difference to me. The stone was a bit rough at the edges but, mostly, it was smooth.

I was the leader and speaker at another retreat several years later. The weekend was going well but, after a full day, I needed some time to myself. It was a clear November night as I walked outside and through the woods. The moonlight was exceptionally bright and, as I stopped in a clearing and looked up at the moon, I was struck by its unusual brightness and clarity, making it appear as a clear, golden disc. Then a thought struck me, *"the moon isn't really that smooth. It's cratered and strewn with rocks and dirt"*, and I sensed God's voice responding, *"But you're seeing the moon as I see you"*. What encouragement! God knows the truth about me – all of the truth – but he also sees me as he means me to be. I too know the truth about myself, but the past is forgiven, and the dazzling light of God's love shows what he is making of me.

Resilience (the strength that enables us to persevere) can't be taken for granted. Just as we need to clean our walking shoes, pump up the tyres on our bike, and maintain our car, so too we must maintain ourselves – body – mind – and spirit. We can't keep running on empty, and an important element of our maintenance is to recognise our own needs. On one occasion, when Jesus was walking along with a large crowd jostling him, he stopped and asked, *"Who touched me?"* [2]. He had sensed power leaving his body as one woman amongst that throng reached out and touched his robe with an unspoken prayer for healing. Jesus sensed her need, and he also recognised the effect the miracle had on his own reserves. On another occasion, after he had miraculously fed a huge crowd [3], he sent his disciples away so he could spend time alone in prayer. Jesus was conscious of his own needs and made a point of maintaining his strength. We too need to care for ourselves, giving our bodies the food, sleep, and exercise they need, and maintaining our spiritual strength through regular prayer and bible reading – not out of a sense of duty or obligation, but because we need it. We are not invincible. Resilience comes when we admit to our vulnerabilities and make deliberate choices to refuel and rearm ourselves.

The Church is a key resource that can help us persevere. Companionship helps us to keep our feet on the right path. We need to nurture relationships that support our sanctification. Although we ultimately stand before God alone, progress in the Christian life is always an "us" matter. We never really do it alone. Even when no human companion stands with us, we still have the Holy Spirit to strengthen and support us. Let's do it *together*.

But there's one aspect of the church that can work against holiness – because it provides an audience. On our own, we tend to do what we want. When we have an audience, we are tempted to act to impress. Ananias and Sapphira [4] pretended to make a valuable gift to the early church in Jerusalem, but they lied about what they were giving. Other church members had received commendation for their large donations, and this couple wanted similar honour. Lying was bad, but their motive for giving was wrong in the first place. They weren't motivated by love, but by a desire to be noticed and admired. Jesus focussed on the issue of giving when he urged his disciples to be secretive about their generosity, but it's appropriate to be shy about every good work that we do. If our aims are pure, we don't need to advertise our goodness. On the other hand, how should we interpret this saying from the Sermon on the Mount?

"In the same way, let your good deeds shine out for all to see, so that everyone will praise your heavenly Father." [5]

How can the Father be praised for our good deeds unless they are visible? The point is to let the deeds speak for themselves, not for us to boast about them. But what if we have mixed motives? In truth, that probably happens much of the time. Every child wants to receive affirmation and encouragement, and the child we once were still lives inside us. We may do our good deeds modestly, but we may also secretly hope that they're noticed. So, when someone thanks or praises us for the things we've done, let's not proudly point upwards, declaring that it's all for God's glory. Let's smile meekly, say "thank you", and inwardly thank our heavenly Father who knows that, though we are now adults, we still need encouragement. Encouragement is an important function of the fellowship. When we encourage one another, we make a vital contribution to the cause of personal holiness.

The encouraging experiences I described at the start of this chapter were high points in my spiritual life, but there have also been many difficult times. I used to think of myself as resilient, and it seemed to be true as I successfully survived a wide range of troubles at various stages of my life. But, at a time when I was reeling from a barrage of unjust and hurtful criticisms, and simultaneously recovering from a debilitating bout of flu, I was hit with another shock. We can often cope with individual problems but, as other issues pile in, their combined effect can crush us. This time it was even harder to take, because one of my sons died, following an operation. I was on the verge of a breakdown, which felt something like vertigo, as if I were standing on a cliff edge and the ground was shaking. I wasn't as strong as I thought. I was as vulnerable as anyone else, and I felt helpless. On the morning when I heard that my son had died, I was booked to provide prayer ministry at our church's Coffee Shop. I could have backed out but decided to go anyway. Instead of providing support, I needed support myself – and someone was there to help me. I found comfort and relief – but the whole experience of seeing and acknowledging my vulnerability was an important step forward. People suffer worse things than I have and come through strongly, but I had discovered the limits of my resilience. To acknowledge one's vulnerability is to be humbled, and that's a good thing. Humility is an important element of holiness.

None of us wants to face trials, but they are part of ordinary life. Perseverance isn't a matter of avoiding life's problems but working through them. Our marriage vows remind us that life contains better and worse times, richer and poorer situations, sickness and health, death and parting. We can sink under the weight of the tough experiences, or we can rise above them, using then as lessons to develop increasing resilience. Perseverance, or what used to be called longsuffering, is a vital part of the Fruit of the Spirit. Thank God for the lessons, and for every encouragement that God sends us.

My late friend and former mentor, Maurice Smith, told a story of his breakdown at a time when he was going through huge problems in his family. His condition was so bad that he was committed to a psychiatric hospital. The discouraging thought came to him, "*I shouldn't be here. Christians don't have mental breakdown.*" That's not true, of course, but he felt condemned. He fell to his knees and prayed, "*O God, I'm a failure*", and he sensed the familiar, reassuring voice of God, saying,
"*Don't worry Maurice,*
You've just discovered my hobby –
I collect failures."

It was during that time of my life when I came close to breakdown, that I wrote this note that I use in my prayers:

> *Holiness comes at a cost. Strong powers range themselves against me, but God is using these forces to squeeze out imperfections and to ensure that my small forward steps don't become occasions for pride. Holiness costs. But I'm not going to give up.*

I was coming to the realisation that, despite all my gaffes and failures, I really, *really*, wanted to go the whole way with God. It reflected the sentiments of a verse that we used to sing in school – lines from John Bunyan's hymn, *"He who would valiant be"*:

> *There's no discouragement*
> *Shall make him once relent*
> *His first avowed intent*
> *To be a pilgrim.*[6]

I also use the following prayer in recognition of the value of all my experiences as a Christian, the joyful ones, and the difficult ones:

> Father, you have led me through sad places,
> Given me experiences I never wanted to face,
> And sorrows I hoped to avoid ~
> But I thank you for them all,
> Because they tested and stretched my compassion.
> Keep leading, testing, and teaching me,
> Because I want a compassionate heart.

Sanctification is a long and testing process with a glorious goal.

Our contribution to the process is to *want* it.

---

[1] *Genesis 3:7-9*

[2] *Mark 5:41; Luke 8:45*

[3] *Matthew 14:21; Mark 6:14; Luke 9:14; John 6:10*

[4] *See Acts 4:32 – Acts 5:11*

[5] *Matthew 5:16 (NLT)*

[6] *From the book, "The Pilgrim's Progress", by John Bunyan – published in 1684*

8. Not Guilty

God's aim isn't to crush us with guilt – ignore Satan's false accusations – memory isn't reliable – the unforgivable sin –ups and downs – Grace isn't rationed and doesn't run out. – don't let guilty feelings continue unchecked.

How do you measure up to your ideals? Not sure? Why do you say that? Is it that you *feel* inadequate – or even guilty? Guilty feelings are all too common among Christians, despite our stated belief in a Gospel of Grace. It's a subject on which we too easily become discouraged. There's a simple rule that can free us of unnecessary guilt. Before condemning ourselves, we should ask what those nagging feelings are demanding of us. If we're being called to repentance, what is it that we need to repent of? What sin is it that needs forgiveness? Precisely what have we done wrong – and I mean *precisely*. To confess something, you need to know what it is that you've done, and that you really did do it. God plays fair. He doesn't convict people of sin just to make them feel bad. His aim is not to crush us under a load of guilt, but to lead us to repentance and forgiveness. When the Holy Spirit convicts, he convicts us of something specific so that:

> "... *if we admit our sins — make a clean breast of them — he won't let us down; he'll be true to himself. He'll forgive our sins and purge us of all wrongdoing.*" [1]

When, on the other hand, we have a generalised feeling of guilt, be assured that the feeling does not come from God, but from the Accuser (that's the meaning of the name, "Satan"). If our sense of guilt is nonspecific, we can't confess it – so, trust God's   Grace and ignore the false accusations. Grace has dealt with our past sins, and we can face the future with confidence.

A familiar New Testament story offers a helpful analogy for this lesson. As Jesus and his disciples were preparing for their final meal together, Jesus took off his coat, put a towel round his waist, and set about washing the disciples' feet. In that culture it was normal for visitors to be offered that service as they entered a house. They needed it because their sandaled feet would be dirty from the unpaved roads. The job would normally be done by a servant, which is why Peter objected to Jesus doing such a menial task.

But Jesus said, "*If I don't wash your feet you don't belong with me*".

Peter replied, "*in that case, don't just wash my feet, but my head and my hands as well*".

Then Jesus responded, "*a person who has already had a bath only needs his feet washed*" [2]

– and that's where we stand in relation to guilt. When we were converted, we were washed clean from our past sins (as illustrated by baptism) but, as we pick up the street-dirt of life, we need to be further cleansed from those individual sins *as and when the Holy Spirit convicts us*. When we receive forgiveness, we start out clean again – every time.

Guilty feelings feed on memories, but memory is not as reliable as most people believe. Experienced interrogators know that, when two witnesses agree in every detail, it doesn't confirm the facts, but suggests that they have compared notes and agreed on a story.

If one witness says that the criminal wore a brown jacket, while another is convinced that the jacket was black, it's not that one of them is lying. Our memories are vague outlines with occasional bursts of apparent clarity. Many people who lived in Britain in 1953 have clear memories of watching Queen Elizabeth's coronation in colour on television – but there were no colour TV broadcasts in 1953! False memories are common, and they can be dangerous. Some people carry a guilty fear that they have committed a crime – even a murder – and that includes me. I had a dream that was so realistic as to be indistinguishable from a past memory. It troubled me for several nights until I logically reviewed the evidence (or rather the lack of it) and realised that it was a false memory. I know I'm not alone in having had that fear, because others have told me of similar anxieties. Simple, logical reflection cleared my guilty feelings away. Beware of being deceived into unnecessary guilt.

Many people have been distressed by the fear that they might have committed "the unforgivable sin", though they are usually vague about what that sin might be. However, the Bible is specific about it. When Jesus talked about an unforgivable sin, it was after some Pharisees accused him of performing miracles by the power of the Devil (who is called *Beelzebub* in this story [3]). But, of course, the source of Jesus's healing power was not the Devil, but the Holy Spirit. By calling the Holy Spirit the Devil, Jesus's accusers were effectively writing off the one power that could bring them forgiveness. In other words, they were writing off their own forgiveness and shutting themselves away from Grace. If ever you fear that your sin cannot be forgiven, just ask yourself, "*do I* **want** *God to forgive me?*". If the answer is "*yes*", you are open to the Holy Spirit, and anything can be forgiven. "*If we confess our sin, he is faithful and just to forgive us our sin and to cleanse us from all unrighteousness.*" [4]

Most of us carry emotional wounds resulting from childhood experiences. As we develop emotional maturity, many of us learn to recognise the source of those worries and put them behind us. Prayer and counselling often help. Childhood wounds may have quite trivial causes – scarcely remembered events that our infant minds misinterpreted. We may have blamed ourselves for troubles that upset us, though we were not responsible at all. Those forgotten experiences may have left us with sadness and unexplained guilty feelings that weigh us down and defeat us. This type of guilt is deceptive, and hard to break free from. Don't seek forgiveness when what you really need is comfort and healing. If sin is the problem forgiveness is available in abundance – but, if you don't know of a specific sin in your life, forget about forgiveness and seek sympathetic, healing prayer.

Human emotions are unstable. We all experience ups and downs but, for some people, the downs are especially extreme. Many of us have remarked that we felt depressed, by which we mean that we felt sad; but clinical depression is far worse than mere sadness. I can't talk from experience about true depression, but I have known unexplained sadness. I used to have prolonged, though mild, bouts of sadness, which I eventually realised were happening around the same time every year – winter. It was the condition known as

Seasonal Affected Disorder (SAD) and is prevalent in higher latitudes where exposure to sunlight is reduced during winter. A common solution for this is to take Vitamin D supplements – and that's a clue to the nature of much emotional and mental disorder. We are physical beings who are affected by physical factors such as body chemistry. Chemistry is a fundamental of our existence; digestion is a chemical process, and poor diet can have dramatic effects on our mood. But body chemistry is a medical matter and not a reason for self-blame. Some Christians, unfortunately, take the view that *"Good Christians don't get mental illness"*. That's not true. We are open to every illness that can inflict a human body – and our mind is contained in our body.

Saintly people can suffer depression. I gratefully remember wise mentors whose lives influenced me for good, but who occasionally suffered forms of mental illness. Some greatly admired Bible characters exhibited traits that may have been depression. Elijah ran away to the wilderness in despair, wishing he were dead [5]; then he went to the mountains, complaining bitterly, ready to throw in the towel and abandon his calling [6]. Many people regard him as the greatest prophet in the Old Testament, but his behaviour exhibited characteristics of depression. The most prominent Apostles in the New Testament, Peter and Paul, each had bouts of melancholy. There is no shame in stress, depression, or any form of mental illness. If this is your problem, seek professional help, and seek prayer – but don't feel guilty.

Don't re-engage in a battle that has already been won. From time to time, you may be reminded of past sins, maybe issues that you fought with for a long period, but which have already been dealt with. You repented, you stopped doing, thinking, or saying whatever it was, and you may even have sought prayer and counselling over the problem. But though you obtained forgiveness and put the matter behind you, it has popped into your mind and created fresh fears and feelings of guilt. Don't engage with it. When God forgives, he really forgives. It is gone. You are in the clear. Such temptations are designed to discourage you – but don't let them. To focus on the accusation is to give it unwarranted attention. Simply refuse to listen and ask the Lord to deal with it on your behalf.

Sometimes, however, it's really hard to get rid of the memory of some past sin, and it keeps coming back to mind – haunting you – though you know you dealt with it long ago, and you have been forgiven. Maybe it's something from before your conversion, maybe back in your teenage years when you were struggling with the challenges of increasing independence. It's in the past, but the memory still troubles you. In that event try this – address the accusation directly – "Yes, I agree, I did that, but I repented and was forgiven. There's no point in reminding me. It's past, forgiven, and buried. I'm not listening!"

Someone may ask, *"Is guilt always negative?"* and, of course, it has a legitimate function when we are guilty of something, and its purpose is to lead us to repentance. It is like fear, which usefully prepares us to run away from danger, but can crush us when it becomes irrational or turns into phobia. The root of inappropriate guilt may lie in childhood when we perceived distressing incidents as punishments that we believed we must have deserved. Children are good recorders of events, but poor interpreters, so they are often harmed inadvertently by innocent actions of their parents or other carers (it is practically impossible to be a perfect parent!). The Church may fail to deal effectively with these emotional/psychological problems so that, instead of new converts receiving a gospel of Grace they absorb a burden of law, which reinforces their childlike fears. Christianity sometimes fails. But God didn't invent a religion called Christianity; he gave us a special gift called Grace.

Grace is always there for us. It isn't rationed. It doesn't run out. If we do something wrong, whether in thought, word, or deed, forgiveness is available – and the time to confess is now (that is, the moment we realise that we have sinned). Immediate repentance brings immediate forgiveness. If we have harmed another person by our sin, we may need to sort it out with them – and the time for that is also now. Whether they forgive us or not is between them and God, but we don't want the issue to remain on our conscience. If we need to make practical restitution, that also needs to be started without delay. There's no need to be obsessive about these things. Our need is simply to clear our hearts and our heads of any guilt that hinders our journey to holiness.

As a monk, Martin Luther had a keen sense of guilt that drove him constantly to confession and penances. Maybe that's why his passion for the doctrine of *Justification by Faith* made him uncomfortable with the book of James. Anyone who was as plagued with guilt, as he was, would feel it as a deep, abiding pain. But Grace is powerful beyond anything we could wish for.

Grace washes away guilt, and it can take away *feelings* of guilt.

Let's talk about feelings because that's the level at which unnecessary guilt often strikes. Human feelings are unreliable guides. We are influenced by weather, by the food we've eaten, by tiredness, by the season, by the news, by what other people have said – and our moods vary from day to day for no apparent reason. Shakespeare said "*there's a tide in the affairs of men*"[7], but it's not just our external affairs that are tidal – our inner feelings ebb and flow. We shouldn't ignore our feelings because they are necessary survival instincts. Feelings can warn us of approaching danger or give us the first signs of illness. They can save our lives. Intellect without emotion is cold, hard, and lame. Emotion without intellect is an untamed animal. We need both – and we need them to be in balance. We should not take feelings as reliable indicators of our spiritual health but, when uneasy feelings arise, we do well to check on our health – physical, mental, and spiritual. If you want to know how you stand before God, ask him – and listen for his answer. Look at his promises. Hear the encouragement – or the warnings – of other believers.

> "*We urge you, our friends, to warn the idle, encourage the timid, help the weak, be patient with everyone.*"[8]

Don't allow feelings of guilt to continue unchecked. If you need forgiveness, it's always available. Otherwise, be encouraged. As the apostle John said – you can overcome the world.[9]

Sometimes we waver between triumph and despair. We feel wonderful when the light of Grace becomes overwhelmingly and delightfully real – until it fades in a fog of discouragement. We are pulled this way and that, just as Paul said:

> "*I have discovered this principle of life—that when I want to do what is right, I inevitably do what is wrong. I love God's law with all my heart. But there is another power within me that is at war with my mind. This power makes me a slave to the sin that is still within me. Oh, what a miserable person I am! Who will free me from this life that is dominated by sin and death? Thank God! The answer is in Jesus Christ our Lord.*"
> [10]

The battle goes on until we become exhausted, and that's the point where we reach the real breakthrough. The mediaeval writer of '*The Cloud of Unknowing*' offers this tip:

> "*When you feel utterly exhausted from fighting your thoughts, say to yourself 'It is futile to contend with it any longer', and then fall down before them like a captive or a coward.*" [11]

Give up. Stop trying. Don't worry. If God wanted you to feel guilty after offering you all that Grace, that would be his problem. Since he clearly does not want you to feel guilty then it's still his problem. If Grace is the answer, then there's no point in searching for different answers. The complex problem of guilty feelings is an issue of un-learning ideas that have become habituated in some of us. We don't need a new gospel for this, nor a new teaching, nor a new technique. We know the right answers, so let's give the problem over to the Lord, and get on with living!

Feeling guilty and don't know why?

Over to you, Lord!

[1] *1 John 1:9 (MSG)*
[2] *John 13:1-10 (speeches paraphrased by me)*
[3] *Matthew 12:31-32, Mark 3:28-30*
[4] *1 John 1:9 (KJV)*
[5] *1 Kings 19:3-4*
[6] *1 Kings 19:10-14*
[7] *From Julius Caesar by William Shakespeare*
[8] *1 Timothy 5:1 (GNB)*
[9] *1 John 4:14*
[10] *Romans 7:21-25 (NLT)*
[11] *From "The Cloud of Unknowing" (anonymous)*

9. Scope for improvement

Since God calls us to be holy, it must be achievable – Jesus overcame temptation with tools we can use – we sometimes sin, but we're not bound to sin – lessons from Eden – the Law teaches us how to sin! – discipleship isn't just a change of beliefs, but a new life – sin isn't inevitable.

Temptation, sin, repentance, forgiveness – temptation, sin, repentance, forgiveness… must we keep riding this carousel round and round and getting nowhere? Is that really what the Gospel is about? Imagine that you are a football manager briefing your team before a match. Your opponents have had a good season so far, and you need to spur your team to play at their best. Will you tell them that they're bound to lose? If you did, how do you think they would perform?

How did our manager – God – brief us for our journey of faith? He urged us to "*be holy*", and if he is calling us to holiness, it must be achievable. He doesn't ask us to do the impossible. But has anyone ever lived a sinless life? The answer, of course, is "yes" – Jesus lived his whole life without sin. The trouble is that a large proportion of the people who believe in Jesus don't really think of him as a man. They focus on his divine nature and presume that he was only able to be free of sin because of his divinity. The Incarnation is far more wonderful than that. When the Son of God took on a human body, he became fully human. He wasn't half divine and half human. He was fully divine and fully human. What's more, he didn't use any tricks or take any short cuts. He submitted himself to the risk and indignity of becoming a helpless baby and going through all the trials, troubles, and temptations of a normal childhood. As a man, he had a mission to redeem humanity by becoming a perfect sacrifice. To be an effective sacrifice, that perfection needed to be *human* perfection, and it was – as Scripture says:

> *"He committed no sin, and no deceit was found in his mouth."* [1]

Jesus didn't win the struggle against sin as the King of Heaven, but as the Son of Man, for *"God is never tempted to do wrong, and he never tempts anyone else."* [2] His victory was a human victory. The fact that the man, Christ Jesus, was without sin, means that a human has achieved holiness. Furthermore, he passed his victory on to his followers:

> *"... take heart, because I have overcome the world."* [3]

The strength to overcome is his continuing legacy to us:

> *"every spirit that does not acknowledge Jesus is not from God. This is the spirit of the antichrist, which you have heard is coming and even now is already in the world. You, dear children, are from God and have overcome them, because the one who is in you is greater than the one who is in the world."* [4]

The above statements contradict assumptions that are widely held within the Church. It is a common belief that we are merely "miserable sinners" and always will be. That isn't a complete Gospel. It isn't an *effective* Gospel. Even the Old Covenant promised forgiveness, albeit through burdensome and repetitive animal sacrifices. The New Covenant was supposed to promise much more, as Jeremiah prophesied.[5] Don't misunderstand me. I'm not saying that we will be able to claim perfection in this life for, *"if we claim to be without sin, we deceive ourselves*" [6]   But there's a big difference between recognising that we sometimes sin and expecting to live a life of constant sin. We are not bound to sin.

The Christian doctrine of *Sanctification* may seem to be opposed to the Christian doctrine of *Original Sin,* but both teachings have sometimes been stretched beyond their proper meaning. The term *Sanctification*, which is certainly used in the Bible, doesn't signify a dramatic "second blessing", as some sects have taught – but it *is* miraculous. It's as much a product of Grace as forgiveness and redemption – but it takes place over a lifetime. The Holy Spirit's power helps us to advance in holiness as we continue our walk with God. Even the Old Testament provides precedents for that prospect. One of the earliest saints, a man called Enoch, walked with God so closely that he escaped death and moved directly into God's presence[7]. The prophet Elijah, a more familiar Old Testament character whose weaknesses are also faithfully reported, became so acceptable to God that he was taken up in a chariot of fire[8] – also avoiding death. Their salvation was by faith, just as ours, but their faith-life was a process of ongoing improvement.

The doctrine of Original Sin can feel threatening. The phrase "*Original Sin*" doesn't appear anywhere in the Bible, and the Church thrived for over 300 years without knowing that expression[9]. But that doesn't mean that the doctrine is baseless. It is standard teaching in most denominations of the Church. But its over-application has inflicted unnecessary fear, distress, and defeatism. Be clear about this – you will not be punished for sins committed by your ancestors. That is specifically ruled out by the prophecies of Jeremiah and Ezekiel:

> *"When that time comes, people will no longer say, 'The parents ate the sour grapes, But the children got the sour taste.' Instead, all those who eat sour grapes will have their own teeth set on edge; and they will all die because of their own sin."* [10]

> *"The Lord spoke to me and said, "What is this proverb people keep repeating in the land of Israel? The parents ate the sour grapes, But the children got the sour taste.' "As surely as I am the living God," says the Sovereign LORD, "you will not repeat this proverb in Israel any more. The life of every person belongs to me, the life of the parent as well as that of the child. The person who sins is the one who will die."* [11]

Humans engage in vendettas, exacting revenge on their enemies' children. God doesn't. Nor will God condemn infants who die without having been sprinkled with water by a priest. That abhorrent interpretation was refuted by Jesus himself:

> *"Take heed that ye despise not one of these little ones; for I say unto you, that in heaven their angels do always behold the face of my Father which is in heaven."* [12]

God's justice is irreproachable. When it is interpreted in its harshest firm, the doctrine of *Original Sin* may seem cruel and unreasonable, so let's look back at its beginning.

A wise monk, commenting on the Garden of Eden story, said it is *"The truest story that I know"* [13], by which he meant that it's beyond doubt that mankind is a fallen race. Some people take the Genesis story as literal history, while others take it as a parable, but it's possible for it to be both at the same time. Some of the parables that Jesus told described ordinary, everyday events and activities – probably countryside activities that he had observed around the village where he grew up. Whether we view the Genesis story as history or as a parable, there must have been a point when humanity became aware of moral alternatives and made the wrong choice. Morality is not an issue in the animal kingdom – a cat feels no guilt about torturing a mouse. At some point in human history, we learnt to feel guilty. The Genesis story focuses on guilt, and we need to ask, "*what does it teach us*?" Looked at as a parable, the style of the story is consistent with other biblical examples, such as Jeremiah's visit to the potter's workshop (almost certainly a real event [14]) or the story of the ewe lamb that Nathan related to King David (a tale that Nathan admits he made up himself [15]).

To interpret a parable, we need to examine its elements to see which parts are important. Many people have focused on the 'forbidden fruit', but we are hardly told anything about it…

- What colour was it?
- What did it taste like?
- Could you peel it or slice it? (even if knives existed back then!)

(**N.B.** There is nothing in the account to identify the fruit as an apple.)

Compare that with the details the book of Exodus gives us about the miraculous food (*Manna*) that the Israelites ate in the desert – "*…it was like coriander seed, white; and the taste of it was like wafers made with honey*".[16]

But look at the information we **are** given in the Genesis story and see what emerges…

- The "Garden" was enormous, reaching out to the Tigris and Euphrates valleys.[17]
- There were only two people in this vast garden.[18]
- It contained trees of all kinds, of which many were fruit trees.[19]
- The one tree that was forbidden was right in the middle of this garden.

Perhaps our focus should be the setting rather than the fruit?

The forbidden tree was placed so prominently that it was sure to be noticed. Was this some kind of 'set up'? If the forbidden tree had been placed randomly somewhere deep in the forest, what were the chances of Adam and Eve finding it by accident and eating its fruit? But, when the tree was placed in a central position that was specifically pointed out, how much did the chances increase? The story illustrates how Law works and sets the scene for later teaching about a better way under the New Covenant [20]. Paul had strong words to say about the negative side-effects of the Law:

> *"Don't you remember how it was? I do, perfectly well. The law code started out as an excellent piece of work. What happened, though, was that sin found a way to pervert the command into a temptation, making a piece of "forbidden fruit" out of it. The law code, instead of being used to guide me, was used to seduce me. Without all the paraphernalia of the law code, sin looked pretty dull and lifeless, and I went along without paying much attention to it. But once sin got its hands on the law code*

and decked itself out in all that finery, I was fooled, and fell for it. The very command that was supposed to guide me into life was cleverly used to trip me up, throwing me headlong. So sin was plenty alive, and I was stone dead. But the law code itself is God's good and common sense, each command sane and holy counsel." [21]

But Paul also saw a solution:

"I've tried everything and nothing helps. I'm at the end of my rope. Is there no one who can do anything for me? Isn't that the real question?

The answer, thank God, is that Jesus Christ can and does. He acted to set things right in this life of contradictions where I want to serve God with all my heart and mind, but am pulled by the influence of sin to do something totally different." [22]

Mankind discovered morality and made the wrong choice, and each of us has made the same mistake in our own lifetime. Most of us try to live decently, recognising the Law, but constantly disappointing ourselves. Law is clumsy and ineffective. As Paul pointed out, the Law actually teaches us how to sin. When we struggle against sin we fail again and again. Paul expressed his feelings about it in a cry of frustration, "*Who shall deliver me from this body of death?*", then he answered himself, "*I thank God, through Jesus Christ!*" Jesus provided the solution. What the law could not do, the Grace of our Lord Jesus Christ did with abundance, and continues to do in those who believe.

The Law failed to bring about righteousness, but there is another way – and it was foreseen long before New Testament days. Jeremiah predicted that the New

Covenant would not be written on stone, but *on human hearts* [23]. The Law speaks to us harshly, telling us what we *must* do, and provoking rebellion. Grace speaks with generous love, changing what we desire by *attracting* us towards the One who loves us. Many churches have the Ten Commandments displayed on the wall, sometimes on ornately decorated boards. People walk past those boards again and again without noticing them. It's easy to ignore a notice, but it's hard to ignore an inner compulsion flowing from the centre of your being. Becoming a disciple of Christ isn't just a matter of changing our mind about the facts. It's not merely a change of beliefs, but the start of a new life.

> *"... anyone who belongs to Christ has become a new person. The old life is gone; a new life has begun!"* [24]

The rules haven't changed – they have moved inside and taken residence in our hearts!

So, life begins again – spiritual life. Don't expect, though, that conversion produces instantly mature Christians. Of course, it doesn't. We enter this new life following the pattern set by Jesus, who started as a baby, knowing nothing, and learning as he grew. Growing as Christians, we encounter many trials and challenges, and sometimes we get things wrong. We don't have to get it wrong. Jesus didn't. However, we do stumble and trip up along the way. That's a pity, but God made provision for it. We can come back to him repeatedly in repentance and receive his forgiveness. Must it always be that way? Are we obliged to wind through life's journey, endlessly circling through sin, to shame, to repentance, through forgiveness, then back into sin again? Surely there must be a way to step off this roundabout!

It is true that everybody has been guilty of sin, "*for all have sinned*" [25], but we have already noted one exception who was as human as you or me. Jesus had the power to resist temptation and he can empower us too. The apostle John had some useful observations on this subject. As he pointed out, if we claim to be without sin, we would be liars[26]. On the other hand, if we *expect* to keep on sinning, we would be denying the power of God. John said:

> "*My dear children, I am writing this to you so that you will not sin. But if anyone does sin, we have an advocate who pleads our case before the Father. He is Jesus Christ, the one who is truly righteous.*" [27]

Notice that John says, "*if anyone does sin*". John didn't expect the people he was addressing to fail every time. As the above quotation makes clear, John's express purpose for writing his letter was to help his followers to avoid sin. This is not to deny our human frailties, but to recognise the redeeming power of Grace.

The "General Confession", which is traditionally repeated in many churches, can seem depressing:

> "*Almighty and most merciful Father; We have erred and strayed from thy ways like lost sheep. We have followed too much the devices and desires of our own hearts. We have offended against thy holy laws. We have left undone those things which we ought to have done; And we have done those things which we ought not to have done; And there is no health in us. But thou, O Lord, have mercy upon us, miserable offenders. Spare thou those, O God, who confess their faults. Restore thou those who are penitent; According to thy promises declared unto mankind in Christ Jesus our Lord. And grant, O most merciful Father, for his sake; That we may hereafter live a godly, righteous, and sober life,*

75

To the glory of thy holy Name. Amen." [28]

But even that sombre prayer ends with an optimistic line – the hopeful prospect of a *"godly, righteous and sober life."* For some people, that kind of confession conveys discomfort and even guilt. What is this sin that I have *generally* confessed? Rather than confessing a vague generality, let's confess *specific* sin, when we're aware of it, and receive *specific* forgiveness and purification. Lay aside guilt and focus on the achievable righteousness that God promised us under the New Covenant.

Must sin always win?
It's not inevitable.

---

[1] *1 Peter 2:22 (NIV)*

[2] *James 1:13 (NLT)*

[3] *John 16:33 (NLT)*

[4] *1 John 4:3, 4 (NIV)*

[5] *Jeremiah 31:31-33*

[6] *1 John 1:8*

[7] *Genesis 5:24 and Hebrews 11:5*

[8] *2 Kings 2:1*

[9] *The doctrine of Original Sin was formulated by St. Augustine of Hippo, who lived from AD354 to 430.*

[10] *Jeremiah 31:29-30 (GNB)*

[11] *Ezekiel 18:2-4 (GNB)*

[12] *Matthew 18:10*

[13] *Abbot Christopher Jamieson, "Finding Sanctuary", Phoenix an imprint of Orion Books Ltd, ISBN978075382149-7*

[14] *Jeremiah 18:1-5*

[15] *2 Samuel 12:1-14*

[16] *Exodus 16:31*

[17] *Genesis 2:10-14*

[18] *Genesis 2:15-22*

[19] *Genesis 2:9*

[20] *I'm not suggesting that this is the only interpretation of the Garden of Eden story. You may have heard several different interpretations to the parables of Jesus. Parables help us find truths – plural – not to make a singular dogmatic point.*

[21] *Romans 7:8-12 (MSG)*

[22] *Romans 7:24,25 (MSG)*

[23] *Jeremiah 31:33*

[24] *2 Corinthians 5:17 NLT*

[25] *Romans 3:23 (KJV)*

[26] *1 John 1:10*

[27] *1 John 2:1 (NLT)*

[28] *From the Anglican "Book of Common Prayer"*

10. Purpose

Holiness lightens our burden – the greater purpose of the Gospel –
confident in prayer – effective in witness – faithful in service – resistant
to temptation – fruitful – participants in revival – ready to meet the
Lord

By talking about holiness, I'm not engaging in pointless moralising, nor do I want to lay heavy burdens on your shoulders. The aim of this book is to lighten our burden by showing an achievable path to reach goals that most Christians aspire to. I believe that most Christians would truly like to be:

- Confident in prayer
- Effective in witness
- Faithful in service
- Resistant to temptation
- Full of joy and peace
- Participants in revival
- Ready to meet the Lord

So, let's check through the list:

Because of God's Grace we have forgiveness and eternal salvation. That's great for us, but there's an even greater purpose in the Gospel, and we are called to be involved in its completion. When we are righteous, God doesn't get any holier. When we do wrong, God doesn't get any less holy. He is unchanging. He always has been holy, he is holy, and he will always be holy – what's more, he calls us to be holy. So, what good purpose could our holiness achieve?

> Do our righteous acts secure our salvation?
>
> > No. His Grace comes to us free of charge.

Do we win God's favour?

    No. He has no favourites.

Do we get extra gifts of the Spirit?

    No. The gifts of the Spirit are no proof of holiness.

But there really is a greater purpose the Gospel. We receive salvation by the free, unmerited, mercy of God, but we're not saved just to be spectators in God's plan.

"For the creation waits in eager expectation for the children of God to be revealed." [1]

"And I say also unto thee, That thou art Peter, and upon this rock I will build my church; and the gates of hell shall not prevail against it." [2]

Gates are defensive devices – they have never been known to mount an attack! Jesus wasn't predicting an assault on the Church by hell's gates, he meant that *we* would be attacking *them*. How can we do that? Let's examine the good things we aspire to:

Confident in prayer

Prayer is the means whereby we attack the gates of hell. We've already referred to the passage about the "*armour of God*" [3] where Paul describes our war against spiritual powers, protecting ourselves by wearing God's spiritual armour – and always praying. Notice that word "always". It's clear that we can't always be on our knees, saying prayers. What we're talking about is a life of continuous connection with God, whatever else we may be doing, and a continuous focus on building the Kingdom of God. We are in his army. We have a job to do – we need to be willing to do it – and we need to be equipped for it.

Prayer isn't difficult. But many people feel that they aren't very good at it. That's a deceptive message from the Father of Lies. If you have said that about yourself, then take it back. Don't make agreements with the devil. If you can think, you can pray. Let me stress that point by putting it another way. Can you think (which is talking to yourself)? Then you can also pray (which is talking to God through the Spirit who lives within you). There are many ways to pray, and some of them don't look anything like the classic image of "saying prayers". Each of us must find our own style, depending on our personality. I've written a book that can help you to find your own style[4], and so have many other writers – so make a point of learning what prayer-style works for you. But, whatever your style, one thing that will certainly hinder your prayer is a lack of confidence in yourself, because you feel disqualified by a sense of guilt.

> *"Who may climb the mountain of the Lord? Who may stand in his holy place?*
> *Only those whose hands and hearts are pure, who do not worship idols and never tell lies."* [5]
> *"if our hearts condemn us, we know that God is greater than our hearts, and he knows everything. Dear friends, if our hearts do not condemn us, we have confidence before God"* [6]

Confidence before God comes from having hearts that don't condemn us – hearts, that is, that harbour no shame that might discourage us. Notice how personal this is. We're not talking about our "Sunday best" self – the image we portray to other people. We're talking about the real self that only we know. If there is something in our life that we don't want anyone else to know about, we can't escape the gaze of our own conscience. For our own peace and confidence, we need inner purity. If our hearts do not condemn us, we have confidence, and then we can pray powerfully.

It matters that we understand the point of this. God doesn't require us to be completely holy before he will answer our prayers. If that were the case, we could never be saved, and we could never pray. But, if, even from the depths of sin we call out to him, he will hear us and receive our prayer. The hindrance to effective prayer is not in God, but in us. If we have a lingering worry about some sin we have not yet confessed and put behind us, then our prayers will lack confidence. By keeping ourselves inwardly clean, following the ways of righteousness, and repenting promptly when we do go astray, we clear our consciences and free our minds to live in an atmosphere of prayer.

This is not about saying prayers at a set time of day. It's good to have that habit, but the work of the Kingdom continues around-the-clock. Imagine yourself as a volunteer fireman or part of a lifeboat crew, or mountain rescue team. You put your energy wholly into your everyday work, but something at the back of your mind is always ready to respond when the alarm bell rings. That's what it's like to be constantly in touch with God. We don't necessarily know who is watching us. We can't predict when we may have an opportunity to speak for the Lord. At any time, without warning, we may come across some situation that prompts us to send up an instant prayer to our Father. As soldiers in the Kingdom army, we are on duty at all times – even while we are focused on other activities – be they work, worship, sport, or recreation. Prayer is not just talking to God but being open to him.

Effective in witness

The way we live has a practical effect on the growth of the Kingdom. We are not all called to a special ministry of evangelism, but we are involved in the proclamation of the Gospel. The occasions may be rare when we can talk with people specifically about our faith, but our lives speak volumes every day. Research among people who were converted at public meetings has found that the influence that drew most of those people to come to hear the Gospel was that they were impressed by the lives of Christian neighbours, workmates, friends, or others who they knew. We are living, breathing testimonies to the power of the Gospel – or, at least, we can be. Our righteousness speaks louder than our voices. A transformed life is the most effective testimony for the power of the Gospel.

Faithful in service

What is your calling? Where do you spend most of your daylight hours? The answer to both questions should be the same. Whether you are a pastor or a road-sweeper, a judge or a shop worker, an engineer or a farmer, a scholar, or a care home resident – as a Christian, whatever fills your day is your calling. That doesn't mean that you can't change your job, but –

> *"...whatsoever ye do, do it heartily, as to the Lord, and not unto men."* [7]

Obviously, the same applies to any volunteer work you may be doing – but don't take on so much extra work that obligations to your family suffer, or your obligations to your primary employment. To do that would not be faithfulness.

Resistant to temptation

The ability to resist temptation is a major concern for anyone seeking holiness, so we will cover it in detail in the next two chapters[8].

Full of joy and peace

Joy and Peace are two of the graces listed by Paul as the "Fruit of the Spirit". This subject too deserves a chapter of its own[9].

Participants in revival

I have heard many preachers speak about revival, but one occasion stands out in my memory. In
that meeting I sensed that both the preacher and the audience were over-excited and missing the point. The 'revival' they were yearning for was a time of heightened excitement, laced with a few miracles, bright skies, no problems, and very little reality. I prayed, *"Lord, don't give them what they're asking for!"* – but he wouldn't have anyway, because that's not the real thing. Revivals of the past have been notable for large numbers of people turning to Christ, but that's not how they begin. The word "revival" implies the reinvigorating of something that's already alive. It implies that Christians turn *back* to Christ in repentance and rededication, which is a painful experience for anyone who has been less than wholehearted in their devotion. Why wait to be knocked flat by an overpowering move of the Holy Spirit? Why not return **now** to the love and enthusiasm that we had when we first found salvation?

My heart quickens when I read the New Testament stories of the early Church and the adventures, miracles, and successes of the early apostles. I get excited when I read stories of revivals in past times or in other countries – but why not now? Why not here? I can pray for revival and watch for God to answer that prayer. But there's one place where I can make sure revival happens. I can make a personal choice to live a revived life! God chooses when to provide a miracle, but it's my choice to read the Bible. It's my choice to spend time in prayer. And it's my choice to live righteously, generously, joyfully, and devotedly.

Revival has been characterised as a roaring fire. What is a fire but a mass of flames? You and I can't be an inferno, but we can each be a flame – and one flame can start a conflagration. Revival can be costly. It has sometimes followed, been accompanied by, or provoked persecution. Whether or not that may be, let's be revived in our own hearts, then pray for widespread revival – whatever it costs.

Why is it that many revivals have been so short lived? I have a theory that people burn themselves out by going to too many meetings and staying up too late too often. If we get used to living in holiness, maybe we'll learn to balance the excitement by treating our bodies responsibly!

Ready to meet the Lord

This is the one truly personal aspiration in this list. We are individually accountable for our actions and will one day have to appear in the Court of Christ.

> *"For we must all stand before Christ to be judged. We will each receive whatever we deserve for the good or evil we have done in this earthly body."* [10]

That text may seem to contradict teachings about the durability of our salvation, and verses that assure us that nothing can separate us from God's love [11]. However, the judgement described in the above text is different from the "Great White Throne" of Revelation [12]. Different words are used to describe the judgement Christians will face – nevertheless we will still be called to account for what we have built on the foundation that has been laid for us.

> *"For no one can lay any foundation other than the one we already have—Jesus Christ. Anyone who builds on that foundation may use a variety of materials—gold, silver, jewels, wood, hay, or straw. But on the judgment day, fire will reveal what kind of work each builder has done. The fire will show if a person's work has any value. If the work survives, that builder will receive a reward. But if the work is burned up, the builder will suffer great loss. The builder will be saved, but like someone barely escaping through a wall of flames".* [13]

Fire will not destroy the gold, silver, or precious stones, but wood, hay, and straw won't last the test. We are not on a cruise; we are not called to lie back on reclining chairs watching the scenery go by. There are times when our Shepherd causes us to lie down in green pastures (and only a satisfied sheep would lie on the grass rather than eating it!) But he also leads us beside the still waters and even through the valley of the shadow of death [14]. Until we get there, we won't fully understand what Christ's judgement scene will be like, but I want to have things of value to show on that day. I don't want to be ashamed in his presence. Ultimately, we look forward to spending eternity in God's presence. What could possibly turn us away from that path? Deception perhaps? Or temptation?

A prayer:

> *May I 'be filled with the knowledge of God's will in all spiritual wisdom and understanding,*
>
> *so as to walk in a manner worthy of the Lord, fully pleasing to him,*
>
> *bearing fruit in every good work*

and increasing in the knowledge of God.' [15]

---

[1] *Romans 8:19 (NIV)*

[2] *Matthew 16:18 (KJV)*

[3] *Ephesians 6:12-18*

[4] *"Still Digging – Scratching the surface and plumbing the depths of prayer", ISBN 9-781542-903868*

[5] *Psalm 24:3-4 (NLT)*

[6] *1 John 3:29-21 (NIV)*

[7] *Colossians 3:23 (KJV)*

[8] *"11. How temptation works" and "12. Overcoming temptation"*

[9] *"15. Fruit basket"*

[10] *2 Corinthians 5:10 (NLT)*

[11] *Romans 8:38*

[12] *Revelation 20:11*

[13] *1 Corinthians 3:11 (NLT)*

[14] *Psalm 23*

[15] *Based on Colossians 1:9 (ESV)*

11. How Temptation Works

Desire is the driving force of temptation – tread carefully in the arena of desires – our "rights" seduce and deceive us – don't be misled by the crowd.

Jezebel is a famous name, though few parents would choose it for their new-born girls. She is remembered as the worst woman in the Bible, with a character much like Lady Macbeth. Like Shakespeare's Scottish anti-heroine, she egged on her husband, King Ahab, to commit murder. But the big story of Ahab's trouble began when he was walking alone. He wandered around on his palace roof in the cool of the evening. In the crowded centre of Samaria, his capital city, there wasn't much open ground, but a nearby vineyard provided rural relief amidst the urban scenery. Gazing at the vineyard, Ahab's fancy became a deep yearning, so he determined to buy the plot. Next morning, he sent a messenger to make a deal with Naboth, a second-generation landowner from one of the city's founding families. Naboth wasn't rich, but he wasn't tempted by the king's money. "*I can't sell the family farm!*", he said.

Ahab didn't take Naboth's refusal well. It ruined his day. Then, when Jezebel saw Ahab sulking, she cooked up a scheme to get Naboth arrested and executed under false charges so that Ahab could take over the vineyard. The plot succeeded, and Naboth was executed. Ahab got his vineyard, but his luck ran out from that point. He was killed in battle, Jezebel was assassinated and so were Ahab's male descendants, and the trouble spread into the neighbouring kingdom. The takeaway lesson from this story is that one moment of selfish desire can set off a chain of trouble that may last for generations.

Free forgiveness. Undeserved acceptance. Generous mercy. The Gospel of Christ is unique among religions. It turns upside down the popular, and mistaken, idea that our destiny depends on our good deeds. God's forgiveness, and our future destiny, depend entirely on God's generosity. But that doesn't mean that morality has no part in our faith. Faith, and God's forgiveness come first – then we start a new way of living. After we receive Christ, we *want* to be righteous. We *want* to be like him. However, we continue to live on this earth, with all its difficulties, challenges, and temptations. To truly wear the '*breastplate of righteousness*' we need to understand how temptation works.

I used to wonder how the instruction, "*thou shalt not covet*", made it into the Ten Commandments. Compared with murder and stealing it seemed such a tame offence. After all, who really gets hurt when you admire your neighbour's goat or donkey? But desire is the sinister fuse that leads to an explosion. It's the driving force from which temptations derive their power. It's the handle that temptation grasps. If we are contented with what we have, where we are, and what we're doing, temptation finds fewer handholds. It's not that all desires are sinful. We get hungry, we need love, we value many things in this beautiful world. But desire can be turned into temptation. We have a saying – '*I want it so badly!*' – and that's a clue. If we want something *badly*, it implies that desire is in control. As Christians, we learn to repent and receive forgiveness, but the images, smells, thoughts, and ideas that previously dragged us down remain in our memory as part of our package of risk.

The Apostle John categorised three kinds of desire that can turn into temptation:

> "*For everything in the world – the lust of the flesh, the lust of the eyes, and the pride of life – comes not from the Father but from the world. The world and its desires pass away, but whoever does the will of God lives forever*" [1].

Ahab's story focused on one of these. That glance, which set off a domino tumble of widespread disasters, was an example of "*the lust of the eyes*" (and it had nothing to do with sex). Other biblical examples are King David ogling at Bathsheba [2], Achan spotting valuables in Jericho's ruins [3], Ananias and Sapphira spotting an opportunity to cheat the system [4] and, of course, Eve eyeing some tasty fruit [5]. Eyes are valuable. Most of us rely on sight more than any other sense and couldn't imagine living without it. But our strongest sense can be our greatest weakness when it comes to temptation. Pornography is an obvious example of visual temptation and derives its strength from the wholesome desires that strengthen the bonds of love in marriage. The corruption of sexual desire turns people into objects for selfish gratification, destroys trust, enslaves precious lives, and creates shame. Pornography was a problem in earlier generations when it was just stories in books, but it is now so graphic, prevalent, and easily accessible that it's hard for any of us to escape its tentacles. But escape we must, because its effects are devastating to marriages, families, work relationships, government and our communion with God. Don't be casual about it. It's slave-driver that always demands more.

Each of our senses can be a vehicle for temptation – hearing, smell, taste, touch. When John spoke about "*the lust of the flesh*" he was talking about all kinds of visual attractions. Any of our bodily desires can get out of control, taking us over. Even eating can be dangerous. When medieval churchman warned about gluttony, they were saying that greed can take over our lives and turn us away from our better selves.

Some may wonder, since forgiveness comes just for the asking, why does all this matter? That's like the question that St. Paul raised rhetorically – "*Shall we go on sinning so that grace may increase?*" [6], and the answer, obviously, is "*No way!*" Having received God's mercy, we're forever indebted to him. More than that, we're enlisted into his army to resist every kind of evil – and that doesn't just mean evil *people*. It was Paul again who drew attention to the spiritual powers ranged against us, and our need for the '*armour of God*'[7]. I used to wonder why prayer isn't listed as part of the armour, until it struck me that *prayer is the arena* where battle is fought. The enemy prefers to attack us from behind, choosing areas such as marriage, work, family, church, recreation… but we can prepare those areas by making them places of prayer. We can stash our armour in each potential battlefield and turn them into holy places, blessed by prayer. If we discover some area of our life that's not already covered by prayer… Well, you can guess what to do about that.

Let's stop for a moment and enlarge on the relevance of prayer. In that passage about the *armour of God*, Paul says that we should be "*praying always*". Obviously, we can't be on our knees all day long, but we can have a continuous online connection with God – whatever else we are doing. We can do, and we need to. If we carry with us the constant awareness of God's presence we can shoot of a mental message to him at any moment, as we face the challenges of life – and *he can speak to us*. We can also choose to take the battle direct to the enemy in intercessory prayer. In prayer, we engage with powerful spiritual powers, and we need protection. A vital part of that armour is the "*breastplate of righteousness*". Resisting temptation equips us for spiritual warfare.

Why is temptation so strong? Because it exploits our personalities and aligns itself with our preferences. One person loves football but hates pop music. Another person hates TV documentaries but enjoys birdwatching. We're all different, but our individual desires can draw any of us into trouble. Temptation can begin so innocently – the accidental glimpse of a top-shelf magazine, the casual glance into a showroom, the smell of a bakery, the memory of an advert – it may take many forms. Desire isn't necessarily bad, but we need to view it in the same way as we regard a frozen pond or the edge of a cliff. Tread carefully in this area.

It's important to remind ourselves that temptation itself isn't sin. Being tempted can be deeply disturbing. To be tempted is to be at risk. But temptation is an invitation that we can, and must, ignore and defeat. We can even reduce its power and frequency. We will look into that more thoroughly in the next chapter (12. *Overcoming Temptation*) but let's first examine the third category of temptation – "*the pride of life*" – yet another natural emotion twisted into the unnatural and dangerous. Pride, after all, is distorted self-esteem. We need to value and care for ourselves, but we need a sense of proportion.

The lust of the eyes and the lust of the flesh tend to provoke temptations that work like slippery slopes – we lose control gradually. The pride of life, however, can tip us over the edge almost before we see the problem coming. Pride is a well-disguised source of temptation (*"I'm not proud!"* is our proud boast!) It comes in camouflage. We tend to think of pride as the sin of the powerful, the rich, and the famous but, while we're pointing the finger at them, three of our fingers are pointing back at us. The reason we fail to notice our pride is that we've narrowed it down to the obvious nose-in-the-air caricature. But what if we talk about *wounded* pride? If our pride can be wounded, then it exists! And the forms it appears in are things like status envy, feeling left out or overlooked, road rage, keeping up with the neighbours. Am I stretching the point? No – this is how it works:

You are driving calmly along the motorway and preparing to overtake a large truck when, suddenly, the car behind you accelerates past with his horn blaring, forcing you to swerve back behind the truck, braking furiously – yes, furiously (and it's you that's furious). You teeter on the edge of losing your temper and chasing the offender. It happened so fast that you don't know where the temptation ended and the sin began – or have you, in fact, sinned? It's hard to tell, but there's no doubt that your peace has been disturbed.

You have been promoted and feel good about it. You've worked hard and feel that you deserve recognition. But one of your colleagues feels aggrieved and reacts spitefully. Now it's your pride that's hurt and, before you know it, you've lashed out in retaliation.

Let's reverse that scenario. This time it's the other person who's been promoted in preference to you. The 'winner' is someone you know to be dishonest, bullying, manipulative and – yes, proud. But *your* pride has been wounded

In scenarios like this, the inner urge is to stand up for our rights. Many domestic quarrels are sparked off by the same fundamental issue. When our sense of justice is threatened, our defensive reaction is almost instantaneous – a reflex – and we're in the midst of conflict with little idea how we got there. The Prodigal Son [8] demanded his rights and lived to regret it. Jesus told another story about guests invited to a meal [9] jostling to claim the best seats (the seats that made them look important). Our 'rights' seduce and deceive us.

Pause a moment to consider what are your true rights... The USA Declaration of Independence came up with a very short list. It declared human rights to be "Life, Liberty, and the Pursuit of Happiness". Anything more than that is a privilege. Pride stands on the assumption that we deserve whatever privileges we may have. That provides broad scope for temptation.

Sometimes we are tempted to hold back when positive action is required. That especially applies in social situations. We are part of a crowd – a community that seems to accept us. So, when the crowd starts to do something wrong – for instance, when they start to bully or taunt one person – we hold back, hoping to save face. Our pride, or our anxiety to keep in favour with the crowd, holds us back from doing what is right.

Temptation is a constant of life on earth. There's no escape from it – not in the desert (where Satan confronted Jesus in person), nor in the hermit's cell. But God provides strength, and there are some strategies we can deploy for our own protection. That's the subject of our next chapter.

---

[1] *1 John 2:16 (NIV)*
[2] *2 Samuel 11:2*
[3] *Joshua 7:21*

[4] *Acts 5:1-10*
[5] *Genesis 3:6*
[6] *Roman's 6:1 (NIV)*
[7] *Ephesians 6:10-18*
[8] *Luke 15:11-32*
[9] *Luke 14:7-10*

12. Overcoming Temptation

Using the Breastplate of Righteousness – what am I allowed to do? –
the Holy Spirit doesn't force his will on us – defer gratification –
beware what you see – learn to be contented – think of good things –
keep one another up to the mark

It helps to understand how temptation works, but we also need to know how to overcome it. Yes, we're all liable to fail, but we don't have to fail every time. We need to be overcomers to maintain the "*breastplate of righteousness*"[1], which is part of the "*armour of God*" – that precious layer of protection that equips us to stand for God in a godless world.

I am assuming that you want to do God's will. If you have truly accepted the gift of salvation through Christ, then your core motivation will have changed. The desire to live righteously is a mark of a true conversion:

> *This, in essence, is the message we heard from Christ and are passing on to you: God is light, pure light; there's not a trace of darkness in him.*
>
> *If we claim that we experience a shared life with him and continue to stumble around in the dark, we're obviously lying through our teeth--we're not living what we claim.*[2]

The desire to be good or righteous inevitably leads to questions of what is right, or "*what am I allowed to do*?" That is a question of law, and law invariably gives a confusing answer. The Coronavirus pandemic that started in 2019 showed how different attitudes produce contrasting responses. Confusion indeed! Some people treated the Public Health precautions as guidance to be valued for the sake of health – their own and others'. Others treated the rules as laws to be resisted, or to be complied with grudgingly and sparingly – they were keen to protect their "rights". But our rights are not always best for us. If you step into the road without looking, because a signal says, "CROSS NOW" (or "WALK") and are mowed down by an oncoming car, the motorist has broken the law and you are in the right – but it's you who is in the hospital! The spiritual powers that seek to tempt us don't care about our rights or our safety, so we need protection. But, much as a stab-proof vest may limit the wearer's freedom of movement, the *Breastplate of Righteousness* place limitations on us. Is the inconvenience worth it? Think about it. A tee-shirt is more comfortable to wear than a stab-proof vest, but it won't stop a knife. Wear the breastplate!

The Holy Spirit gives us power to resist temptation, but that doesn't mean that we have no choice. He doesn't force his will on us, compelling us to do the right thing. That would take away our freewill – and he wants us to follow him willingly. So, we sometimes find ourselves in the place of the Prodigal Son, knowing that we have done wrong, dreading the consequences, but recognising that the worst that God will do to us will be better than remaining in the grime and the darkness. So, we trudge slowly homewards with our head down, fearing the process of rebuilding our relationship with the Father. In the parable, the Father doesn't just accept the son – he *rushes* to accept him. This is a distinguished member of the community disgracing himself by hoisting up the skirts of his robe, exposing his legs, and *running*! When we talk of power, we often mean physical strength, but this is the power of example. God surprises us by making himself "*of no reputation*", brushing aside our self-humiliation, and accepting us freely and fully.

How, then, can we overcome temptation?

Start by learning to defer desires – even the harmless ones – so that you build up strength to defeat the bad ones. Is there something you fancy? Put it off and do something else. Make this exercise a habit, until you have learned to be in control. Deferring gratification is a valuable psychological exercise. Choose something which is legitimate and which you enjoy – then give it up for a while. You don't need to deny yourself forever, but long enough to learn that you can control your desires. By such exercises you can increase your contentment and strengthen yourself to face harder challenges. Let me repeat that – increase your contentment, just as Paul advised:

> *"…I have learned to be content whatever
> the circumstances."* [3]

Overcome temptations by denying them the power they derive from desire. Ultimately, the way to defeat the pull of desire is to desire something better – like being God's good and faithful servant.

Beware of what you see. We can't help catching an accidental glimpse, but we can turn away. And we can avoid being in places, or picking up reading matter, or watching media that we know will contain problematic images. We don't need to be prudish about this, and we definitely shouldn't judge other people. We just need to recognise what harms *us* – and take steps to protect our own purity and integrity. These are not rules. They are advice, on the lines of, "*Don't go too near the cliff edge!*" What harms you may be different from what harms me, just as one person's easy jog would be another person's heart-attack risk. Temptation comes custom-made for each individual, so we need to develop a strategy that works best for us. Remember, we are in a war. The enemy knows our weaknesses, so we need to protect ourselves by recognising those areas of vulnerability and taking action to shore up our defences.

None of us can claim to be free of sin, as St. John said, "*If we claim we have not sinned, we make him out to be a liar and his word is not in us*"[4]. But that doesn't mean that we're *obliged* to sin. John also said, "*... if anybody does sin, we have an advocate with the Father – Jesus Christ the righteous one*"[5]. Notice the "if" in that sentence. We have a choice. Start by building life routines that make the 'right road' easier to walk on. "*Make level paths for your feet*"[6]. Strengthen the spam filters on your digital devices, avoid TV programmes or online films that contain scenes that disturb your inner peace, put a brake on the urge to buy, to spend, to pursue your desires. Hold desires lightly and shrug your shoulders when you can't have what you want. Learn to be contented. Most things that you want can wait.

What I've just been saying concerns the ways we self-arm ourselves in advance of temptation; but what can we do when temptation comes to us unexpectedly? To quieten temptations, don't engage with them, because that puts more focus on the temptation. To engage with temptations is to acknowledge them. Don't fight them. Just treat them like the ring of an incoming 'junk' phone call. Refuse to acknowledge them. Don't answer the call:

In distraction or temptation,

> we're not obliged to fall –
> though the phone may keep on ringing,
> we don't have to take the call. [7]

If the battle gets harder, and the attacks don't stop, move the battlefield into the arena of prayer, where you've already stashed your spiritual weapons, and you know that heaven's armies will fight alongside you. That's where you find the truth of James' advice, "*...resist the devil and he will flee from you.*" [8]

Sins of the past can sometimes leave troubling memories, such as images that keep popping back into your consciousness. Don't worry. Memory is not necessarily permanent. Our brains have systems for making 'space' for new memories by forgetting recollections that aren't reinforced. So, don't reinforce disturbing thoughts by dwelling on them. I'm not talking about traumatic memories that your mind has hidden from consciousness, but which still provoke fears and reactions. Trauma needs healing. But there may be past temptations that we dwelt on longer than we meant to, and maybe even succumbed to. Repentance dealt with them, but they still pop unbidden into our thoughts. Don't try to fight them. Rather change the subject and do something else – think about something else. As time goes by, those memories will become less clear and fade away.

Changing the subject to think about "good things" is easier if you have a store of good memories to draw on, so why not stock up? As Christians, we are often encouraged to count our blessings, but we're rarely told why. We'll, here's the reason. Every time you count your blessings you are reinforcing the memory of those blessings. There's no need to be super pious about this.

You don't need to focus exclusively on Bible verses and spiritual songs. Every good memory is worth reinforcing – holidays – family events – walks, runs, and rides – favourite scenes and pictures. Every good image you can easily summon back into consciousness is a handy foil for unwanted thoughts that try to hold your attention. Think on these things.

This is not about self-righteousness or passing judgement on others. It's about putting on *"the breastplate of righteousness"* so we can engage in spiritual warfare. Treat tempting thoughts as if they are unimportant and don't deserve your attention. Look, as it were, over their shoulder, not acknowledging their presence. Act as if you are looking for something else. You are, of course, looking for God himself. By doing this you bring your focus back onto your yearning for God – your desire to love him more than anything else. And by re-focussing on your love, you overcome everything else. If it's still a problem, admit defeat and throw yourself on God. Ask him to take over and fight on your behalf. Allow him to fill your mind with thoughts of his love and mercy.

> When it's all too much
> I fall down like a coward
> and leave it to God. [9]

Our spiritual senses are a vital part of our protection, and we need to keep them tuned in. Temptation doesn't always present itself openly. Deception is its favourite trick. It presents itself innocently or unexpectedly – and it finds plenty of opportunity in the workplace. We don't mean to compromise, and the things that try to draw us to drop our standards often start out by looking innocent. Then, by the time that we see their true nature, we are already partly committed. What is at stake in these cases is usually your honesty and integrity – both too precious to put at risk. As a piece of armour, the breastplate sits over the heart, and our heart is where we may discern the approach of danger. Sense when the quiet murmur of the Spirit is making you feel uncomfortable. Maybe your conscious mind can't see a problem in the trend of what's happening, but your inner peace is disturbed – maybe just a little. Whenever that happens – whenever and however slightly – pause, listen, and ask questions. Fools rush in. A little delay is rarely a problem when you're sincerely seeking to be and to do your best.

Anger is an emotion, a possible source of temptation, and a potential power for good. Many people struggle with a type of anger that surfaces from nowhere in response to almost nothing. It's *unreasonable* anger that wells up from deep within, often provoked by trivial causes. Is it sin? Yes and no. It certainly isn't righteousness, but it may better be regarded as an illness. Others may suffer similar issues but react in an almost diametrically opposite way, internalising the problems as sorrow or depression. These things may be rooted in deep emotional pain coming from childhood experiences or more recent trauma. If you experience those kinds of problem, the solution may not be just repentance, but healing prayer. You may need help and counsel.

But sometimes we feel angry because of injustice, abuse, attack, or other wrong done to us or somebody else. That sort of anger is not a sin – but it can lead to sin. Jesus was angry when he saw the traders defiling the Temple. But he didn't rush to act on his anger. Instead, he went away, sat down, and made a whip of cords to drive out the traders [10]. He didn't let anger overcome him but used reason to work out his response and channel his anger effectively. That's what Paul meant by his advice to *"be angry and sin not"* [11]. Anger becomes a sin when we let it take control. But, if it is a response to unreasonable provocation and we steer it with reason, it can be a power for good. The folklore advice was to count to ten before responding. That's wise, but Jesus must have taken much longer to work out his response, and if we follow his example, we can prevent an appropriate emotion from tripping us into sin.

David used his anger to kill Goliath. Read the story again [12] and notice how indignant David was when he heard the giant's taunts. But David took his anger down to the stream and carefully selected five smooth stones, all the while thinking how he would hit the target in the right place, with the right force to bring the giant down. Anger is a gift from God. It's an emotion that empowers us to act strongly and bravely. The problem is that it has the potential to be dangerously explosive, so we must handle it with care. Pray for wisdom to use this gift at the right time, in the right circumstances, with the right motives.

There's another valuable tool that can help us win over temptation. Although, ultimately, each of us is responsible for our own behaviour, that doesn't mean that we have to accomplish everything on our own. We have our friends in the church:

> *"A person standing alone can be attacked and defeated, but*

two can stand back-to-back and conquer. Three are even better, for a triple-braided cord is not easily broken." [13]

Make a habit of confiding in and praying with a trusted group of friends. A committed group of two or three friends sharing personal challenges, praying together, keeping one another up to the mark, and supporting each other makes each individual stronger to withstand discouragement or temptation. Many churches encourage members to stand together in this way, as 'Prayer Triplets' or TiE Groups (***Three* is *Enough***). It works, provided we are truly honest with one another. If we struggle to overcome a persistent problem, such as uncontrollable anger, and we share that confidence with our trusted prayer-partners, we make ourselves accountable to them, and enlist their prayers in our support.

"Brothers, if someone is caught in a sin, you who are spiritual should restore him gently." [14]

Finally, take control of your thought life by building a positive habit of choosing to focus on good things –
"Finally, brothers and sisters
Whatever is true
Whatever is noble
Whatever is right
Whatever is pure
Whatever is lovely
Whatever is admirable
If anything is excellent or praiseworthy
Think about such things." [15]

---

[1] *Ephesians 6:14 (NIV)*
[2] *1 John 1:5-6 (MSG)*

[3] *Philippians 4:11 (NIV)*
[4] *1 John 1:10 (NIV)*
[5] *1 John 2:1 (NIV)*
[6] *Hebrews 12:13 (NIV)*
[7] *Quoted from my book, "Still Digging – Scratching the surface and plumbing the depths of prayer"*
[8] *James 4:7 (KJV or NIV)*
[9] *Another quote from "Still Digging"*
[10] *John 2:13-17*
[11] *Ephesians 4:26*
[12] *1 Samuel 17:1-51*
[13] *Ecclesiastes 4:12 (NLT)*
[14] *Galatians 6:1 (NIV)*
[15] *Philippians 4:8 (NIV)*

13. Victorious

*Hitting the mark – conversion's inner changes become obvious – our
ability to live righteously – the temptation of Jesus wasn't a pointless
charade – the Son of God risked everything – each trial makes us
stronger.*

In the New Testament, the Greek word that is
translated as 'sin' has the sense of 'missing the mark'.
Forgiveness covers the times we have missed God's
standards and then repented. But once we have
experienced God's Grace, we have a much stronger
yearning to hit the mark. We *want* to do what's right –
and we can. As we lift the bow, and put the arrow in
place, our Saviour's arms reach round us, his hands grip
our hands, and he directs our aim. In the words of
John Newton's famous hymn, "*'twas Grace that brought
me safe thus far, and Grace will lead me home*" [1]. Grace first
forgives our past sins, removing whatever barrier was
keeping us from experiencing God's presence, then it
empowers us with a new life-force. Positive Grace
gives us the power to do the good, which our hearts
want to do. St. Augustine put it this way: "*Him that wills
not, Grace comes to meet, that he may will; him that wills, Grace
follows up, that he may not will in vain.*" [2] That translation
may not seem much clearer than Augustine's original
Latin! But read it again slowly. A believer who
sincerely wants to do good is followed up by God's
Grace, which bestows the power to do good.

In the City of Jericho, there was a man who collected
taxes on behalf of the unpopular ruling power. You
probably know the story. His name was Zacchaeus.
Like most tax collectors at that time, he took every

opportunity to line his own pockets as he gathered in the money. He was unpopular and deserved to be. But, when he heard that Jesus was coming into town, he climbed up a tree to get a good view. Imagine his surprise when Jesus walked right up to that tree and called him down. There's more to the story, but I'll go straight to the end, when Zacchaeus repents of his wrongdoing and determines to put it right by repaying all that he'd stolen. His life had changed completely. I have come across many stories like that as I've seen people became Christians and had their lives turned around. The inner change (their conversion) became obvious from the change in their outward behaviour. They *want* to do what's good and right. If that's not your conversion experience I urge you to go back to the beginning and commit yourself wholly and sincerely. God is always available to a returning Prodigal.

Never underestimate the power Christians are given to resist sin. James assured us that, if we resist the devil, he will run away from us [3]. We come to God humbly, acknowledging our sinful past, but we come to him with confidence, gratefully believing that he's made provision for our success. The apostle, John, had a lot to say about our ability to live righteously:

> *"No-one who lives in him keeps on sinning. No-one who continues to sin has either seen him or known him. No-one who is born of God will continue to sin, because God's seed remains in them; they cannot go on sinning, because they have been born of God." [4]*

> *"Dear friends, if our hearts do not condemn us, we have confidence before God and receive from him anything we*

ask, because we keep his commands and do what pleases him." [5]

"We know that anyone born of God does not continue to sin; the One who was born of God keeps them safe, and the evil one cannot harm them." [6]

So, although we will probably never know in this life that we have reached the point of holiness *and will remain there*, it is neither pride nor boastfulness to aspire to such a condition. Rather, it's faith that God has given us the tools and the right and authority to use them. Peter believed this too:

"His divine power has given us everything we need for a godly life through our knowledge of him who called us by his own glory and goodness. Through these he has given us his very great and precious promises, so that through them you may participate in the divine nature, having escaped the corruption in the world caused by evil desires. For this very reason, make every effort to add to your faith goodness; and to goodness, knowledge; and to knowledge, self-control; and to self-control, perseverance; and to perseverance, godliness; and to godliness, mutual affection; and to mutual affection, love. For if you possess these qualities in increasing measure, they will keep you from being ineffective and unproductive in your knowledge of our Lord Jesus Christ." [7]

These tools and powers were tested and proven long before we were born. Initially, they were tested in one of the earliest characters of the Bible:

"It was by faith that Enoch was taken up to heaven without dying – 'he disappeared, because God took him.' For before he was taken up, he was known as a person who pleased God." [8]

The import of that story is that Enoch lived an exemplary life. I don't think it's stretching the point to say that he was holy by the time that God took him. The Bible doesn't give us a complete life story for Enoch, but we must assume that he started out as a normal child. We are told that he grew up to become a father, and his notable period of "walking with God" seems to have followed that. He was regarded as a prophet [9], and probably his goodness developed gradually as he grew older. It is certain, however, that by the end of his days, he was "*a person who pleased God*". We referred to Enoch in an earlier chapter, where we also considered the prophet Elijah. Both men reached such a point of holiness that they somehow bypassed death and were swept up into the presence of the Lord. To describe these two cases as exceptional would be an understatement of enormous proportions! Apart from these two scarcely explained exceptions, out of the billions of people who have ever lived, everyone ends up by dying. However, there are other people who stand out from the Bible record – others like Moses, who sometimes earned God's displeasure, but ended up being remembered as "*the man of God*" [10] – others like David, whose sin is recorded in embarrassing detail, but who ended up being remembered as a "*man after God's own heart*" [11]. Though our past record may be poor, it's still possible to exchange it for God's "*Well done!*"

The Bible speaks of another man who definitely pleased God and received a "*Well done!*". The passage that tells that story is very familiar. It was the occasion when Jesus was baptised in the River Jordan, and a voice from above said, "*This is my beloved Son, in whom I am well pleased.*" [12]. We know that Jesus was good – so good, in fact, that he could face his enemies and say, "*Can any of you prove me guilty of sin?*" [13]. But his sinless life could not be taken for granted. Following his baptism, when Jesus went into the desert and was tempted by the Devil, it was not a pointless charade. Satan wasn't gambling against a double-headed coin. There was a genuine risk that the man, Jesus of Nazareth, would give way to temptation – but he didn't, as later writers confirmed:

> "*This High Priest of ours understands our weaknesses, for he faced all of the same testings we do, yet he did not sin.*" [14]

This is an incredible concept, but the biblical record shows that Son of God really did risk everything by becoming a human. Never forget that Jesus lived his life on earth *as a man* – not as a stage act, but in stark reality. The primary tool that he used to counter Satan's temptations was one that is readily available to us – the words of Scripture that he had learnt since childhood. Jesus was born as a human baby, with the need to learn everything, just as each of us has done.

> "*Even though Jesus was God's Son, he learned obedience from the things he suffered.*" [15]

How could it be possible that Jesus had to *learn* obedience? I don't believe that he was ever DISobedient, so what does this mean?

Jesus told a parable about two sons whose father spoke, first to one and then to the other, asking them to work in his vineyard [16]. The first son refused, but later relented and obeyed his father, the second said "yes", but didn't go. When Jesus was praying in Gethsemane, he asked that the Father would "*take this cup from me*" – he knew how terrible an ordeal he had to face, and he shuddered at the thought. He could have escaped – but he went through with it. Let's pause for a moment and review that statement. Jesus could have escaped. The arrest took place in darkness in a wooded garden. The guards who had been sent to make the arrest couldn't identify their target without the help of Judas. Jesus didn't live in the Jerusalem area; he was only a visitor. The guards hadn't seen him on TV! They weren't carrying his photo on their smart phones! If Jesus chose to, he could have made an escape in the darkness. When, after his arrest, he was brought before Pontius Pilate, the Governor tried to find an excuse to release him – if only Jesus would say the "right" words – but he wouldn't. Although Jesus was the Son of God, with the authority to call on angelic help (as he said himself [17]) – but he didn't make that call. Read the gospel accounts in detail and see how many chances Jesus had to get out of trouble. His obedience was voluntary. There is a type of obedience that is slavish and legalistic, and there is an enhanced obedience that thinks through the full implications of the command, then chooses to obey. Jesus was the son who recognised the seriousness of his Father's calling and chose to obey. Let's follow him.

Not only has God provided us with the power to be righteous, but he has left us with the freedom to choose. That's risky. Tyranny might have been easier, but God has no wish to over-ride our will. He wants us to be one with him by our own choice. When we first made the choice to follow him most of us found it easy, because it was new and exciting. Then, over time, we lost that first glow, and the way may have seemed harder. That wasn't accidental. God allows it so that we learn to stand on our own two feet. As we progress further, we discover that we learn more in the tough times than we learn on the peaks of rejoicing. It's in the challenging experiences that we are shaped into the people he wants us to be. Each trial makes us stronger, and every period of apparent dryness sharpens up our

awareness of the Lord and our ability to follow him.
We may stumble from time to time, but he looks on us
as we look on a child learning to walk. We rejoice as we
see our children repeatedly getting up and trying again –
and God rejoices over us. Through it all, he continues
to accept us and to hear our prayers.

> *"Don't you see how wonderfully kind, tolerant, and patient*
> *God is with you? Does this mean nothing to you? Can't you*
> *see that his kindness is intended to turn you from your sin?"*
> [18]

The incredible truth is that God believes in us! The
Son of God believed in us enough to die for us.
Despite knowing our weakness, he still believes in us
enough to give us freedom of choice. He believes, in
fact, that we will succeed – even though we doubt
ourselves. We have freedom, but we are never more
free than when we submit fully to him. Paul, speaking
of Israel, compares their attempts to "*establish their own*
righteousness" with the believer's opportunity to submit
to God's righteousness [19]. Our aim is submission to
Him, rather than showing off to Him or to a human
audience. Our power is not in bravado but in Grace.

Most religions demand that you keep the rules in order
to earn divine acceptance. The Christian Gospel offers
free forgiveness and acceptance, then gives you the
power to keep the rules. That's good news – I mean
really good news! This power turns the
Commandments into Promises:

    – you *shall not* murder
    – you *shall not* steal
    – you *shall not...*

Keeping the rules, or rather, doing God's will, is not a way of earning his favour, but thanking him for it. His love wins our hearts, so we want to love him back, and the way to express our love is to obey him – and his commandments are not hard. Psalm 119 finds 176 ways to affirm that truth, but they can all be summed up in one word – love. That's why one frequently used Anglican prayer describes service for God as "perfect freedom"[20].

> "*Therefore, since we have these promises, dear friends, let us purify ourselves from everything that contaminates body and spirit, perfecting holiness out of reverence for God.*" [21]

> "*Now may the God of peace, who through the blood of the eternal covenant brought back from the dead our Lord Jesus, that great Shepherd of the sheep, equip you with everything good for doing his will, and may he work in us what is pleasing to him, through Jesus Christ, to whom be glory for ever and ever. Amen.*" [22]

God gives us the power to be victorious.
Let's use it wisely and deliberately.

---

[1] *From the hymn, "Amazing Grace", by John Newton*
[2] *Written by St. Augustine of Hippo in A.D. 426 or 427.*
[3] *James 4:7*
[4] *1 John 3:6, 9 (NIV)*

[5] *1 John 3:21-22 (NIV)*
[6] *1 John 5:18 (NIV)*
[7] *2 Peter 1:3-8 (NIV)*
[8] *Hebrews 11:5 (NLT)*
[9] *Enoch's son was Methuselah, the oldest man in the Bible. Methuselah's name is believed to mean, "when he dies it shall come", and Methuselah died in the year of Noah's flood.*
[10] *Deuteronomy 33:1*
[11] *Acts 13:22*
[12] *Matthew 3:17 (KJV)*
[13] *John 8:46 (NIV)*
[14] *Hebrews 4:15 (NLT)*
[15] *Hebrews 5:8 (NLT)*
[16] *Matthew 21:28*
[17] *Matthew 26:53*
[18] *Romans 2:4 (NLT)*
[19] *Romans 10:3*
[20] *From the Second Collect for Peace in the Anglican "Book of Common Prayer"*
[21] *2 Corinthians 7:1 (NIV)*
[22] *Hebrews 13:20-21 (NIV)*

14. Discipline and Excess

"Don't be too good or too wise!" – self-discipline is good – self-punishment is an unholy counterfeit – moderation is vital – be motivated by love – discipleship is an adventure – discomfort does not enhance prayer

Be wise, be moderate! Hmm... Moderation sounds like a wise idea but, to many minds, it stirs up thoughts of banality, mediocrity, and boredom. That's why extremes have such appeal. Adventure attracts, stirring speeches excite audiences, visionary ideas draw adherents, and even those who earnestly desire to serve God can be lured to seek holiness in ways that are less than the best. Not that adventure, great sermons, visions etc. are bad – but, where possible, we should choose our adventures with care – and the things we listen to. The Bible contains this surprising text:

"So don't be too good or too wise! Why destroy yourself?" [1]

Yes, it really says don't be too good (or, as the King James version puts it *"Be not righteous over much"*!) Is it suggesting that you should moderate your murders? Does that mean that it's OK to steal provided you don't take too much? Obviously not! What it means is, don't be fanatical. Even the search for holiness can be taken to excess, and examples of that can be found quite early in church history.

The early Church in imperial Rome was frequently under persecution, but not continuously. It came in waves, sometimes just in particular regions, and sometimes across most of the empire. Persecution drove some Christians to deny their faith while others faced martyrdom with great bravery. Martyrs won such respect that, by the third century, they were often treated as celebrities within the Church. People would visit them in prison and seek their prayers, in the belief that their intercessions had special merit. Infatuated with hopes of glory, some people actually sought martyrdom, provoking the civil authorities by audacious, and sometimes offensive, actions. Their mistaken shows of devotion were distortions of holiness.

Following repeated epidemics in the medieval period there was a widespread belief that the plagues had been sent by God as a punishment. Bands of men, known as flagellants, paraded the streets of European cities beating themselves with whips, hoping to appease God's wrath. Many people regarded those displays as acts of holiness. They were not. Self-discipline is good. Self-punishment is an unholy counterfeit.

Dan Brown, the popular novelist, is not an obvious fan of religion – but he often makes religion a focus of his stories. One character in his novel, *The Da Vinci Code,* is a monk called Silas who is fanatically religious. While he fights for what he believes is right, he punishes himself in the name of piety by strapping on a device (called a *cilice*) that inflicts pain to the point of drawing blood. Silas is a credible character because there really are people who believe that self-harm can be an act of piety. People don't gain spiritual merit by cutting their skin, walking barefoot on jagged stones, burning themselves, or any acts of physical self-mortification. God honours the suffering of those who are tortured by persecutors – but we don't win points by torturing ourselves.

In our search for holiness, we need to beware of the kind of distractions that these stories exemplify. Holiness has been given a bad name because of excesses. Be wise. We don't want counterfeits. We need the real thing. Physical acts of penance don't demonstrate God's generous goodness or glorify Him. Rather, they exemplify the harmful belief that salvation can be earned by our good works. Paul anticipated the possibility of over enthusiastic self-denial in the sublime "love chapter" from 1 Corinthians:

> *"I may give away everything I have, and even give up my body to be burned – but if I have no love, this does me no good."* [2]

Before engaging in any act of self-denial, even a recognised and valued spiritual act such as fasting, we need to ask ourselves, "Where is the love in this?" There is nothing we can do to earn the gift of God's Grace. Grace is bestowed freely on those who simply believe. We could never do enough to earn what Christ has given to us freely. The Christian desire to do good doesn't stem from a belief that we can earn salvation, but from an overwhelming sense of gratitude for God's extravagant Love and Grace.

Jesus told us to love our neighbours as ourselves but, if we don't love ourselves, what chance do our neighbours stand? Driven by love, we may choose to deny ourselves certain pleasures and privileges so that we can benefit others, but self-denial that seeks no benefit for anyone else is simply selfish. Self-denial may involve providing practical help, by giving time, money, or goods that we might otherwise have kept for ourselves. It may lead us to devote time to praying for others. It may lead us to do all kinds of generous acts –

but the acts are godly only when they are motivated by love, which is the true cause, goal, and measure of righteousness.

Holiness is not so much an external matter as it is about our hearts, as Jesus pointedly explained:

> *Then Jesus called the crowd to him and said to them, "Listen and understand! It is not what goes into a person's mouth that makes him ritually unclean; rather, what comes out of it makes him unclean."* [3]

He was responding to criticism by the Pharisees because they saw the disciples eating without observing the ritual hand-washings required by their traditions. We need to beware of making similar mistakes. There is a place for fasting, and other forms of self-denial as aids to prayer and self-discipline, but denying the body doesn't prove inner goodness. We can abstain from chocolate whilst harbouring hatred in our hearts. We can spread malicious gossip, whilst self-righteously clinging onto our glass of non-alcoholic drink.

History remembers many devout women and men who lived lives of self-denial in ways that most modern Christians would consider extreme. Restricted diets, rough clothing, sleeping on stone floors, and living simple lives, without luxuries – many have nobly borne such conditions out of necessity. But it wasn't Elijah's rough clothing, or John the Baptist's simple diet, that marked them out. It was their practical goodness, and their faithfulness to their calling. Each of these people chose their manner of life for practical reasons to suit their calling. They were not trying to secure divine favour but rejoicing in it.

Self-discipline is quite different from self-harm – and a lot safer! But don't be put off by the word "safe". Like moderation, safe doesn't have to be boring. Self-discipline is a valuable way of working out our faith, and it can be part of a great adventure.   Paul explained its role by using an illustration from sport:

> *"Every athlete in training submits to strict discipline, in order to be crowned with a wreath that will not last; but we do it for one that will last for ever. That is why I run straight for the finishing line; that is why I am like a boxer who does not waste his punches. I harden my body with blows and bring it under complete control, to keep myself from being disqualified after having called others to the contest."* [4]

The word "discipline" is related to the word "disciple", which reminds us of those men and women who walked with Jesus during his earthly ministry. Now that's exciting! Discipleship is an adventure that needs the same kind of commitment that an athlete makes to keep winning races. Successful athletes start with a natural ability, but peak performance comes only through commitment.

Self-discipline is the deliberate choice to arrange our lives in ways that maximise our usefulness in the Kingdom of God. Nothing that I'm saying here contradicts the clear doctrine of salvation by Grace through faith. We cannot earn God's acceptance. But we are called to resist enemy forces that have no grace and are opposed to God. The fact that we have been reborn into new life doesn't stop their attacks but makes them more determined to undermine and discourage us. We have privileged access to God through prayer, but prayer only happens when we make time for it. The Bible, often called "the sword of the Spirit", is there to inspire us, but we have to turn the pages (or swipe the screen) ourselves. God's full defensive toolkit is available to each of us, but we must make the choice to use it. Paul urged us to "*put on the whole armour of God*" [5]. He didn't just say that we *have* this protective gear. We need to put the armour on. God provides the helmet of salvation, so let's wear it prominently to protect our minds from distractions. Let's take up the shield of faith, strap on the breastplate of righteousness, and "*Pray on every occasion, as the Spirit leads*" [6]. Our proper objective is a renewed life, evidenced by practical righteousness that makes the world a better place. That's another way of living out the prayer "*your kingdom come, your will be done...*".

As related in the book, "*The Cross and the Switchblade*", a Pentecostal pastor called David Wilkinson felt uncomfortable about the amount of time he devoted to watching television. So convicted was he about this that he got rid of the TV and devoted the time he saved to prayer. Just giving up the TV would have been self-denial. Giving that time to prayer was self-discipline. His prayers focussed increasingly on the needs of his local area of New York, and especially on the youth culture of drug addiction and gang violence. The outcome was a powerful Christian witness that led to many changed lives.

Holiness is practical, and advances in the faith can often be accomplished by very simple steps, like setting the alarm clock a little earlier to allow time for devotions, choosing a location, and making provision for sitting or kneeling in reasonable comfort. Discomfort doesn't enhance prayer, but rather distracts from it. Self-discipline involves deliberate action to support our holy habits and protect ourselves from temptations. Paul said:

> *"Put to death, therefore, whatever belongs to your earthly nature: sexual immorality, impurity, lust, evil desires and greed, which is idolatry. Because of these, the wrath of God is coming. You used to walk in these ways, in the life you once lived. But now you must also rid yourselves of all such things as these: anger, rage, malice, slander, and filthy language from your lips. Do not lie to each other, since you have taken off your old self with its practices and have put on the new self, which is being renewed in knowledge in the image of its Creator."* [7]

Our self-discipline will benefit other people. If we make the most of the gifts God has given us, he will be able to use us more effectively to build his Kingdom. If we surrender some of "our" time, "our" wealth, and "our" rights, we may produce good effects that can reach right across the earth. If holiness is our goal, let's seek it with self-discipline and sincere love.

---

[1] *Ecclesiastes 7:16 (NLT)*

[2] *1 Corinthians 13:3 (GNB)*

[3] *Matthew 15:10-11 (GNB)*

[4] *1 Corinthians 9:25-27 (GNB)*

[5] Ephesians 6:13 (KJV)

[6] *Ephesians 6:18 (GNB)*

[7] *Colossians 3:5-10 (NIV)*

15. Fruit basket

Righteousness is simple – just one commandment – holiness is impossible to fake – goodness is not a mere absence of evil – growth in Grace is an ongoing process – God has given us the power to live rightly

Wrongdoing is complicated. Righteousness is simple. If you don't believe me, look at this catalogue of evil deeds, drawn from Romans 1:29-31 and Galatians 5:19-21:

adultery

backstabbing

boastfulness

carousing (boozing)

deception

depravity

disobedience towards parents

dissensions

drunkenness

envy

factions (divisions)

gossip

greed

hatred

hostilities

idolatry

impurity

insolence

jealousy

malicious behaviour

murder

outbursts of anger

pride

promise breaking

quarrelling

refusal to understand

selfish rivalries

sexual immorality

sorcery

strife

witchcraft

Human ingenuity is constantly devising new ways of doing evil, which is why legislators are under continuing pressure to pass new laws. So, the above is not a

complete list of vices. But the following list *is* complete
– these are the Christian virtues:

- Love
- Joy
- Peace
- Patience
- Kindness
- Goodness
- Faithfulness
- Gentleness
- Self-control

That list, of course, is the nine-fold "fruit of the Spirit"
that Paul wrote about [1]. Simple, isn't it? It really is less
complicated to be righteous – provided you have the
Spirit of God. In fact, it's simpler than that, because
the whole list can be summed up in the first item. If we
have Love, all the other virtues will flow from it.

> *"When you add up everything in the law code, the sum total*
> *is love."* [2]

Just one commandment – could it be any simpler?
Notice too that the fruit of the Spirit is *singular* – fruit,
not fruits. That matters, because the marks of spiritual
wholeness can't be ticked off on a score-sheet awarding
6 points for kindness, 7 for joy, and a miserable 1 for
self-control. If we are being led by the Spirit, the fruit
of the Spirit will show in *all* its aspects. This is what we
really mean by holiness, and it's impossible to fake.
Paul didn't invent the fruit analogy. Jesus introduced it
when he pointed out in his "Sermon on the Mount"
that deeds reveal a person's character – he said, "*you will
know them by their fruit*" [3].

Don't let's get discouraged about this. These are high standards, and we may rightly feel that we have some way to go to reach the best. Fruit doesn't appear full and ripe in an instant. It grows. Trees that produce fruit don't exert obvious effort. Have you ever heard an apple tree straining to squeeze out fruit? Fruitfulness is in the nature of the tree's being. Plum trees produce sweet fruit, lemon trees produce sour fruit, and both are valued. Spiritual fruit can't be faked. So, what should we do? I recommend the following prayer, based on verses from one of Paul's letters:

> *May I*
> *'be filled with the knowledge of God's will in all spiritual wisdom and understanding,*
> *so as to walk in a manner worthy of the Lord, fully pleasing to him,*
> *bearing fruit in every good work*
> *and increasing in the knowledge of God.'*
> *May God strengthen me*
> *'with all power, according to his glorious might, for all endurance and patience with joy,*
> *giving thanks to the Father, who has qualified [me] to share in the inheritance of the saints in light."* [4]

It's appropriate to pray because this is God's business. The fruit of the Spirit can grow in the one who prays because the Spirit lives inside. Fruitfulness won't be produced by our effort, but by our submission.

Notice the nature of this 'fruit of the Spirit'. Some of these virtues can be evidenced in private; but most can only be done with or for other people. Love needs an object. Patience (or, in the older translation, "Longsuffering") implies that someone is nearby to test our patience. Kindness requires a recipient.

Faithfulness suggests that there is a person, or group of people, who need our loyalty. Gentleness is only apparent when someone needs care or protection. You may be unsure whether the Fruit of the Spirit is evident in your life, but your family and friends probably know. You may prefer not to ask them, however!

Holiness is often thought about in negative terms, but goodness is not mere absence of evil (*"I haven't murdered anybody so far today!"*). Holiness is not just avoiding adultery, forgoing theft, ignoring idols, or whatever other harmful thing we've managed not to do. It's whatever positive contribution we have made to the world. It's whoever's lives we've enriched, what value we've given, what light we've brought to people who live around us. The Fruit of the Spirit gives substance to this reality. Love – the core of the Spirit's fruit – is not mere absence of hatred. Love creates life. Love restores broken relationships. Love rights wrongs. Love heals. Love is the ultimate creative force.

Growth in Grace implies change; but doesn't everyone change as they get older? Yes, life changes everyone, but not always for the better. Most of us experience setbacks, and they are often painful. I have a chronic pain condition that arose following a broken arm and is currently in remission. It was painful, but illogical because it started when the fracture was almost healed. The condition is called Complex Regional Pain Syndrome – but it was little understood at the time. That was in the early days of the Internet so, as I learned more about CRPS, I started a website to increase awareness of it. During the 13 years that I ran that website [5] I corresponded with many people who were in extreme agony, and I learnt how differently people respond to pain. Pain drives personalities to their extremes. Some people become kinder and more empathetic, others become angry and aggressive.

Similar differences arise from the aging process. Many people become calmer as they mature. Others become more selfish, more angry, more bitter. Normal life brings changes, but rarely does it bring transformation. With most people, the pressures of life merely moderate or exaggerate the traits they already have. To observe lives that have been transformed, look for people who have found new life in Jesus Christ.

> *"...anyone who belongs to Christ has become a new person. The old life is gone; a new life has begun!"* [6]

Conversion creates a new life, and once a new life has begun, what necessarily follows is growth.

Growth in Grace is an ongoing process, working outwards from the inside, in other words, from the heart. Fruitfulness doesn't come about by desperately trying to be loving, joyful, peaceful and so on, but by nurturing our friendship with the Lord. Part of that nurturing comes through our "holy habits" of regular devotions. But another major part of it comes through the pressures of life and relationships. People can be so trying! Those who are closest to us often test our patience and sometimes seem to bring out the worst in us. That doesn't sound like a route towards holiness, but it is. The pressures of life shape and polish us; they show up our rough edges; they smooth off our blemishes. When life feels trying, say prayers of thanks, because that's part of the process of sanctification. As we thank God for our trials, we make them more bearable. As we thank him, we increase our resilience.

As we thank him, we are submitting to him and discovering his perspective. As we see his perspective, we grow in Grace.

The fruitfulness of our lives depends on our relationship with God himself. By patiently tending that relationship, we nourish the spirit within us and feed the processes that lead to blossoming and fruitfulness.

> *"But blessed are those who trust in the Lord and have made the Lord their hope and confidence. They are like trees planted along a riverbank, with roots that reach deep into the water. Such trees are not bothered by the heat or worried by long months of drought. Their leaves stay green, and they never stop producing fruit."* [7]

Trust – hope – confidence – words of reassurance that remind us of the feelings of comfort and security that children receive when they run to a parent for protection. When we allow the Lord to parent us, when we spend time in his presence, when we become disciples as well as believers – then we become like the tree planted close to the water. We set ourselves up to be fruitful – and it lasts, as Jesus promised:

> *"Ye have not chosen me, but I have chosen you, and ordained you, that ye should go and bring forth fruit, and THAT your fruit should remain..."* [8]

Time appears to sweep things away rapidly, as minute follows minute, but God's perspective is eternal. Things that now seem fleeting will reappear – for instance, our prayers are saved up as precious fragrance to be celebrated in eternity [9]. The fruit of our actions will also be remembered, and I'm talking about the good that we do. When we accept the gift of salvation our sins are washed away. As we confess sins committed after conversion they too are cleansed and forgotten. The foundation of our life in the Spirit has been laid – but what have we built on it?

"...if anyone builds on the foundation with gold, silver, costly stones, wood, hay, or stubble, each man's work will be revealed. For the Day will declare it, because it is revealed in fire; and the fire itself will test what sort of work each man's work is." [10]

The metaphor has changed, but the subject is the same. Fruit has been replaced by the craftwork we have created. If our deeds have crafted works of lasting beauty and great value (like gold, silver, and precious stones) it will survive the test of the fire – but, as for hay or stubble...

"For this very reason, make every effort to add to your faith goodness; and to goodness, knowledge; and to godliness, mutual affection; and to mutual affection, love." [11]

But don't be disheartened, dismayed, or discouraged, because God has given us the power to live rightly:

"His divine power has given us everything we need for a godly life through our knowledge of him who called us by his own glory and goodness. Through these he has given us his very great and precious promises, so that through them you may participate in the divine nature, having escaped the corruption in the world caused by evil desires." [12]

"Therefore, as God's chosen people, holy and dearly loved, clothe yourselves with compassion, kindness, humility, gentleness and patience. Bear with each other and forgive one another if any of you has a grievance against someone. Forgive as the Lord forgave you. And over all these virtues put on love, which binds them all together in perfect unity." [13]

Having wrapped all the virtues up in the one word, "Love", Paul unwraps it again in his famous "love chapter" (1 Corinthians 13) where he breaks Love into its component parts – but these are not rules to be reached by human effort. This describes what love *is*:

- Love is patient
- Love is kind
- Love doesn't envy
- Love doesn't boast
- Love isn't proud
- Love honours others
- Love is not self-seeking
- Love doesn't easily get angry
- When others inflict harm, Love doesn't keep the score, but forgives
- Love doesn't take pleasure from evil
- Love values truth
- Love protects
- Love trusts
- Love hopes
- Love perseveres
- Love doesn't give up
- Love doesn't fail

Look again at that list and substitute the word "Love" for any of the names of our Lord. It fits! Of course, it fits because, as John told us:

God
is
Love [14]

So, how can we become more like God? That seems like a huge question, but the Bible provides an answer that's both simple, and deeply mysterious:

> *"And we all, who with unveiled faces contemplate the Lord's glory, are being transformed into his image with ever-increasing glory, which comes from the Lord, who is the Spirit."* [15]

This is reasonable (that word again) because what we look at, what we think about, and what we desire, changes who we are and what we do. We are transformed as we contemplate the Lord's glory, so let's keep reading about him, thinking about him, talking together about him, dwelling on his goodness, his kindness, his generosity, and his Grace.

Help me, Lord, so to live in your presence that I will be changed from the inside, making my life reflect your goodness and your glory.

---

[1] *Galatians 5:22*

[2] *Romans 13:9 (MSG)*

[3] *Matthew 7:16-20*

[4] *Based on Colossians 1:9-12*

[5] *The website was called "RSD Alert" (RSD being the former name of what was then a little-known ailment). By the time I closed the website the condition was much more widely recognised, and the medical profession was providing much improved information and treatments. My amateur contributions were no longer needed.*

[6] *2 Corinthians 5:17 (NLT)*

[7] *Jeremiah 17:7-8 (NLT)*

[8] *John 15:16 (KJV)*

[9] *Revelation 5:8*

[10] *1 Corinthians 3:12,13 (WEB)*

[11] *2 Peter 1:5-7 (NIV)*

[12] *2 Peter 1:3-4 (NIV)*

[13] *Colossians 3:12-14 (NIV)*
[14] *1 John 4:8*
[15] *2 Corinthians 3:18 (NIV)*

16. The Walk

The journey of faith is a walk – how to stay upright on the narrow path – we are alone and not alone – choosing again and again – when will we know we have reached the goal? – Your Kingdom Come

The meeting was in the ballroom of a large country house in the Lake District. During a quiet moment following a period of singing, a voice from the middle of the crowded room related a mental image (otherwise known as a vision) of a car struggling up a hill, making heavy going of it, with the wheels spinning. After a pause, the same voice laughingly commented *"I think someone's wheels are spinning!"*. Beware of glib interpretations! As another voice pointed out, *"the Christian life is not a ride, but a walk. To follow in the footsteps of Christ, you need to get out of the car and walk."* Walking is slower than driving but, on a rough track, it's surer and safer.

Walking, as a metaphor for the journey of faith, goes right back to the book of Genesis:

"And when Abram was ninety years old and nine, the LORD appeared to Abram, and said unto him, I am the Almighty God; walk before me and be thou perfect." [1]

Walk... and be perfect. That summarises the message of this book.

Let's consider the significance of walking. The walk of a human being is distinctive. As we walk upright on two legs, we can see further than any four-footed animal of equivalent size. That's a significant advantage, and so is the freedom our hands have to hold, carry, and even manipulate objects. It also leaves our mouths free to talk. Walking is a useful ability. But our upright walking has a significant disadvantage. We're quite good at keeping our balance, but compared with most quadrupeds, we're more vulnerable to falling over. To walk safely, we need to use our eyes and tread wisely. I've heard it said that our inner struggle between right and wrong is like walking a tightrope. But we're not walking a tightrope. We're walking the narrow path that Jesus spoke about:

"small is the gate and narrow the road that leads to life, and only a few find it." [2]

Yes, the road is narrow, but it's broad enough for us to walk confidently. There's not room for us to walk the path arm-in-arm with others. We can have people ahead of us, and people following behind us, but we're each ultimately responsible for our own walk with God. And that's the enigma about this solitary walk. We are alone and not alone for our Lord promised to be with us each step of the way. The steps of our walk consist of continual choices – choices to refuse evil – choices to do good – choices to continue following in the Master's footprints – choices to recommit to him again and again:

Choosing Again

"From this time many of his disciples turned back and no longer followed him. 'You do not want to leave too, do you?' Jesus asked the Twelve. Simon Peter answered him, "Lord, to whom shall we go? You have the words of eternal life." [3]

Years ago
I chose to follow Jesus.
Day by day
I make that same choice again.
Choosing him

Is always the answer for me,

Though my choice
Is in the face of doubt
Though my choice
Is in the face of suffering
Though my choice
Is in the face of pain.

Hopes may rise,
And hopes may be battered down,
But each time
I find no better answer
Than to stay with the friend who never fails.

We desire holiness and press toward that goal, but will we know when we have reached that point? Despite the story I related at the start of this chapter, let me change the metaphor back to a car journey that isn't quite over. You know if you've had a crash or a breakdown and, if you did, you remember calling the emergency services and the help you received. You're aware of any close shaves or hold-ups that happened along the way. Maybe nothing like that happened. You may have enjoyed a perfectly smooth drive up until now. You know how things have gone so far. But you can't say, "I've made it", until you come to the end of your journey.

Now, about revival...

Your Kingdom Come

"This, then, is how you should pray ...
your kingdom come, your will be done,

on earth as it is in heaven."
Matthew 6:9-10 NIV

"Your Kingdom come"
Is not a dream of realms beyond the sun,
Where angels sing
And all is good and God's will's always done.
NO! It's a call for massive change -
"Your will be done ON EARTH"
Let earth and heaven be rearranged.
Bring righteousness to birth.
It's not a helpless cry to God
For him to spring to action.
It's a willing offering of self
For our participation.
So now I say "your Kingdom come"
And mean just what I say.
And say the more "your will be done -
Lord, start the work in me."

---

[1] *Genesis 17:1 (KJV)*
[2] *Matthew 7:14 (NIV)*
[3] *John 6:66-68*

Acknowledgements

Though it may seem strange, I want to begin by thanking people I would be best not to name. I'm thinking of people who made my life difficult, people who cheated me, people who criticised me unfairly (in my view), people who tried to oust me from management positions (the business world can be cruel!), people who undermined me, accused me, deceived me, or hurt me in any way. I thank them because, though they may have meant harm, God turned it for good. The tough experiences of life shave off our roughness and help us to properly assess our worth. I thank God for every one of those people and the part they played in making me who I am.

But, of course, I am also grateful for the many people who helped, supported, and encouraged me. Love is the most important lesson they taught me – and that can't be learnt from a book. My wife, Kathleen, has seen my worst moods, my sorriest lapses, my weaknesses and, yes, my triumphs too – and has remained loyal to me for almost 60 years. My sons and their families have brought me joy, as have many friends, some of them for very many years. I am deeply grateful for two special men, Ted Hubbard and Maurice Smith (both now deceased) who I looked up to as mentors at earlier stages of my life. Also, for six exciting years, it was my privilege to share in the work of evangelism as a member of the sixties Christian rock band, "*The Pilgrims*", and I'm grateful to my fellow band members, two of whom are still alive, for sharing that adventure with me (www.pilgrimsmusic.co.uk). Those six years were foundational to my journey of discipleship and set the scene for much that was to follow.

Obviously, as I gained life exposure, I still needed support and encouragement, so I'm grateful to all those who shared in my experience of church in Bromley, Lanes End, Vigo Village, and Spalding. Most especially, I thank the members and leaders of St Michael's Church, Stoke Gifford (www.stmichaelsbristol.org) which has been my spiritual 'home' since 1999. I particularly thank Louise Pott (a member of St Michael's) who read an early draft of this book and raised many helpful suggestions and questions, also Tony Goodman (formerly of "*The Pilgrims*" and, subsequently, a missionary and pastor) who challenged my thinking with searching questions. We need people who we can trust to be honest with us.

Other books by Derrick Phillips

Little Church of Bethany
"*Small village – big heart – huge influence*"
In first century Palestine, a little village called Bethany was home to a family whose lives of faith helped change history. In 20th century Britain an 800-year-old village church went into decline, much like many at that time. But it reversed its decline and grew to become a force for change in the local community and beyond. *Little Church of Bethany* weaves together these two stories, focusing on Bethany's characters and events and showing the power of small churches to change themselves and their community.

Pilgrims Rock!
"*The true story of the first Christian Rock Group*"
Amplified music, electric guitars, drums, and songs with a beat are commonplace in 21st century churches, Christian conventions, and evangelistic events – though some people still deplore their presence. Before the 1960s such things were unthinkable. Times have changed. But how did it all start? The beginnings can be found in a suburban living room, where a young Bible student's short sermon produced 100% success. Everyone in the room was converted – all four of them. That night forms part of the history of the first Christian rock band – and the rest of the story is just as remarkable.

Prophecy in Today's Church
"*A compact study of a valuable gift*"
(Co-author Revd. Canon Simon Jones)
Prophecy has been a crucial support to faith since the earliest times – and it still matters in today's church. But prophets need nurture, encouragement, support and accountability. This study answers key questions that matter for individual prophets and the churches where they serve.

Still Digging
"Scratching the surface and plumbing the depths of prayer."

Prayer is for all of us – extroverts, introverts, active people, those who enjoy stillness, folk who love solitude, and individuals who hate being alone. ***Still Digging*** validates a variety of ways of praying, so that everyone can feel confident to pray ***as they are***.

The short chapters of ***Still Digging*** cover the needs of those who are just starting out in prayer, and those who sense God's call to go deeper, in intercession or contemplation. But we're all on the same journey. We can't reach the deeps without paddling through the shallows.

SOS – Stumbling Over Scripture
"A journey from fundamentalism to faith"

Fundamentalism is a risky strategy for maintaining faith. It can lead to arrogance or even cruelty and it doesn't cope well with doubts. This book records the author's 20-year journey from fundamentalism to honest faith, facing the problems and questions that cause people to stumble over scripture.

About the author

Derrick Phillips became a Christian in the 1950s and initially planned to enter the Christian ministry – a plan that changed after he received an experience with the Holy Spirit and a call to evangelism as a member of *The Pilgrims* – a 1960's Christian rock band. After leaving the band, Derrick began a career in corporate management and eventually formed his own business. At the same time, he served in various roles in local churches, wherever he was living at the time. He is now retired. He has served in church leadership, written, and published several books and articles on the faith and served in musical ministry as a guitarist and singer. Derrick publishes articles and poems and runs a personal blog. He lives near Bristol, where he is a member of St Michael's Church, Stoke Gifford.

www.derrickphillips.co.uk

www.derrickjohnphillips.blog

Printed in Great Britain
by Amazon